Healing the Father Wound

A Women's Bible Study through the Gospel of Mark

Carolyn Rice

Alarias Press LLC

Copyright © 2022 by Carolyn Rice

Published by Alarias Press, LLC

All rights reserved.

No portion of this book may be reproduced in any form without written permission from the publisher or author, except as permitted by U.S. copyright law.

Scripture quotations marked with NKJV are taken from the New King James Version®. Copyright © 1982 by Thomas Nelson. Used by permission. All rights reserved.

Scripture quotations marked with NLT are taken from: *Holy Bible*, New Living Translation, Copyright © 1996, 2004, 2015 by Tyndale House Foundation. Used by permission of Tyndale House Publishers, Inc., Carol Stream, Illinois 60188. All rights reserved.

Scripture quotations marked with NIV are taken from THE HOLY BIBLE, NEW INTERNATIONAL VERSION®, NIV© Copyright © 1973, 1978, 1984, 2011 by Biblica, Inc.® Used by permission. All rights reserved worldwide.

Scripture quotations marked with ESV are taken from The ESV® Bible (The Holy Bible, English Standard Version®), copyright © 2001 by Crossway, a publishing ministry of Good News Publishers. Used by permission. All rights reserved.

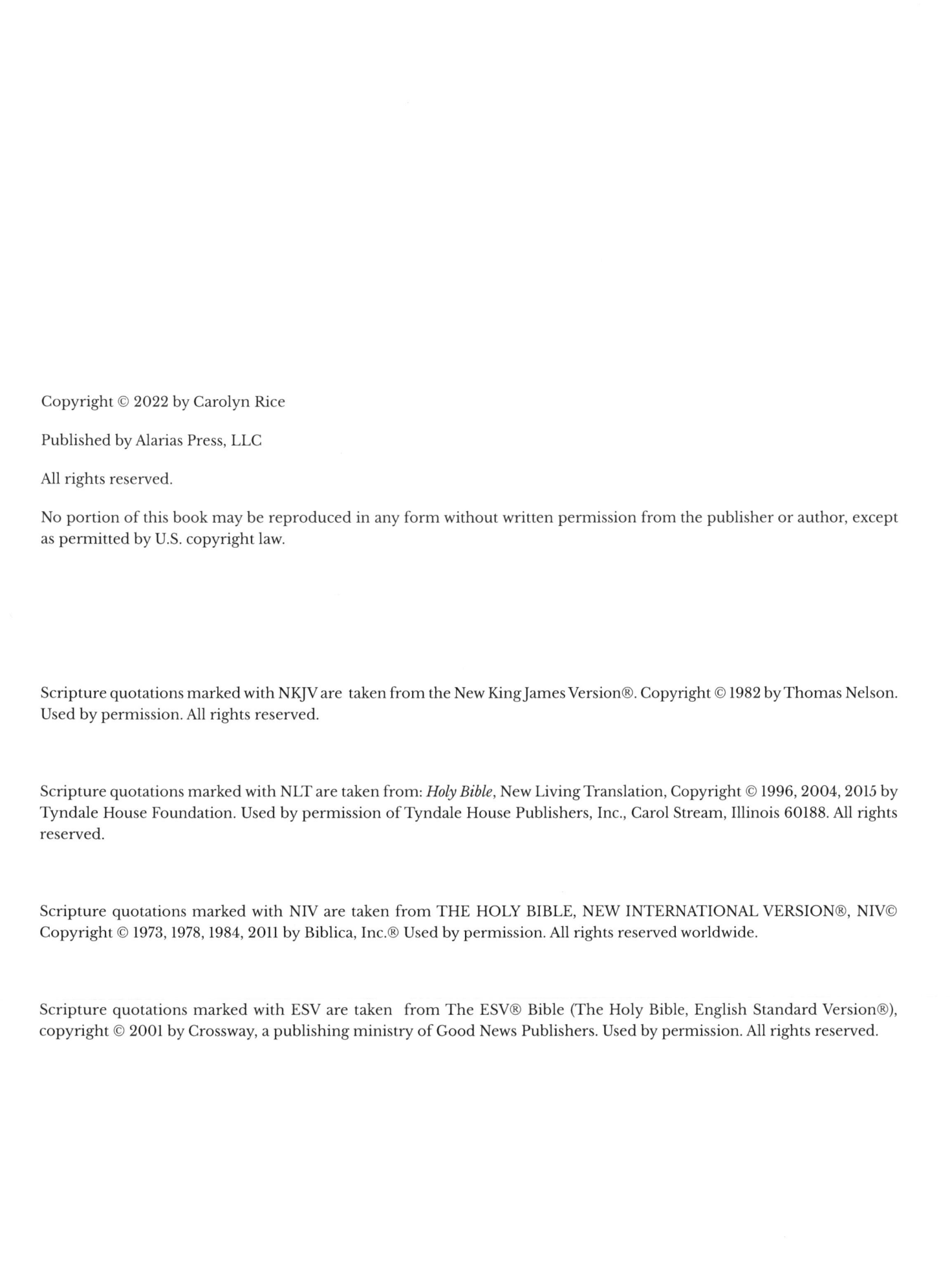

Contents

Acknowledgements — VII
Introduction — IX
— XI

1. Day 1 — 1
2. Day 2 — 7
3. Day 3 — 13
4. Day 4 — 19
5. Day 5 — 23
6. Day 6 — 29
7. Day 7 — 33
8. Day 8 — 39
9. Day 9 — 49
10. Day 10 — 55
11. Day 11 — 65
12. Day 12 — 73
13. Day 13 — 83
14. Day 14 — 89
15. Day 15 — 97
16. Day 16 — 103
17. Day 17 — 109
18. Day 18 — 115
19. Day 19 — 123
20. Day 20 — 129

21.	Day 21	135
22.	Day 22	139
23.	Day 23	143
24.	Day 24	149
25.	Day 25	155
26.	Day 26	161
27.	Day 27	167
28.	Day 28	173
29.	Day 29	183
30.	Day 30	191
31.	Day 31	195
32.	Day 32	201
33.	Day 33	207
	Also By Carolyn Rice	215
	Did You Love This Bible Study?	217
	About the Author	219
	Prayer for Salvation	221
	Resources	223

Acknowledgements

To my husband Lyle. Without your support, encouragement and prayers, this book would not have been written.

To my wonderful prayer team who has interceded for every part of this book, from beginning to end. I am so very thankful for your prayers over me, this book, my podcast, and the things going on in my life at the same time. From the bottom of my heart, I am so incredibly thankful for each one of you.

To my readers. I love your emails, your comments and your encouragement. They truly do help me see that it is all worthwhile when you share your heart like you do.

To my Heavenly Father. Thank you for making yourself real to me.

Introduction

"If you feel you have been birthing something in prayer, please stand up." The pastor said.

I felt like I should get up, but I wasn't sure if he was talking about me, although my heart was pounding.

Several people in the congregation stood.

It must be them, I thought, while my heart continued to pound.

"The woman who's still seated, but your heart is pounding, you need to stand up too."

My husband smiled at me, as if he knew I was supposed to stand up the whole time.

I rose from my seat, and as I looked at the man up front, I saw anger flash across his face. This shook me, and as he prayed for people, I wasn't sure how to respond to him.

I was sure he was angry at me.

After we got home from church that day, I felt a prompting to go watch the replay of the service, especially the part where I felt I saw anger.

And as I watched, to my surprise, there was no anger there at all, only sincere compassion on his face. I played it again, and again, never seeing anger in the replay.

But I'd been so *sure* I saw anger!

That's when I felt the Lord speak to my heart. The anger I saw was not from this man who prayed for me, and who had prayed for me specifically. The anger I saw was from a father figure who I'd grown up with. Somehow, I had put the anger I grew up with on this man who stood in a place of authority.

And to show me this truth even further, this man came into my husband's and I's lives in a special way, and we really got to know him. He became an example to us of what a godly, loving father is supposed to be like. He is caring, sincere, and authentic in his faith.

The Lord showed me through this experience that when we've been through traumatic experiences, or grown up with men who were angry and abusive, often we can see other men in authority in the same light, simply because they represent a father figure.

Later, I realized I had seen my Heavenly Father through these same lenses, and I came to know my Heavenly Father in a new and different way.

John 14:9 says that when we've seen Jesus, we've seen the Father. I wrote this Bible Study especially to take a look at Jesus, how He interacted with people, what He felt for them, and to give a picture of what our Heavenly Father is like through looking at the actions of Jesus.

My prayer for you as you go through this study is that you will begin to experience your Heavenly Father in a new and different way and begin to heal from the wounds inflicted on your heart by any father figure who didn't represent fathering well.

May God bless you as we dive into the Word of God together.

Love,

Carolyn

He who has seen me has seen the Father

John 14:9 NKJV

Day 1

Read Mark 1:1-28

What do verses 2-3 say John's purpose was?

What were Simon and Andrew doing when they met Jesus? (Verse 16)

Write out Mark 1:17:

Notice what Jesus calls Simon and Andrew to do first.

And after they do it, what does He say He will do?

What does this show you about what Jesus will do as you follow Him?

Have you ever felt like you had to get yourself together before you could truly follow Jesus?

What did this verse speak to that?

Who else did Jesus call to follow Him? (Verse 19)

And what was their response to Jesus? (Verse 20)

Who did Jesus meet in verse 23?

What did this man cry out?

What was the condition of this man?

What was this man's condition *after* an encounter with Jesus? (Verse 26)

Based on the reading of this section, what observation can you make about what Jesus wants for people?

What truth about Jesus stood out to you from this passage?

John 14:9 says when you've seen Jesus, you've seen the Father. What does this show you about your Heavenly Father?

What's going on in your heart as you realize this?

Write or say a prayer receiving this truth about your Heavenly Father and asking Him to heal the places you've been hurt by father figures in your life. You can use my prayer below as an example if you wish.

Prayer

Father God, I receive the truth about You that I've learned from Scripture, and I ask that You'd make this truth real to me. Help me to know You in this way as My Heavenly Father. Father, I choose to forgive (my father figure) for acting in ways that were not becoming of a father, or for not even being there at all. I pray, Father God, that you would bring healing to my heart and life from the wounds this father figure inflicted. In Jesus' mighty name, I pray, amen.

Day 2

Read Mark 1:29-45

In verse 30, what was the condition of Simon's Mother-in-law?

Describe her condition *after* an encounter with Jesus. (Verse 31)

Who was brought to Jesus in verse 32?

In verse 34, what did Jesus do?

In the morning, describe where Jesus went and why. (Verse 35)

When Simon and those who were with him came looking for Jesus, what was Jesus' answer to them? (Verse 38)

Specifically, what was the purpose Jesus spoke about?

As Jesus was preaching, what did He cast out? (Verse 39)

In your own words, summarize what happens in verse 40-45.

What was Jesus' response to the leper in verse 41?

What was the condition of the leper *after* an encounter with Jesus? (Verse 42)

In that same verse, what was Jesus moved with?

Is there an area of your life that you have cried out to Jesus about? Explain.

Write again what Jesus said to the leper about being willing.

What does this passage speak to your heart about Jesus' willingness to work in your situation?

What truth about Jesus stood out to you from this passage?

John 14:9 says when you've seen Jesus, you've seen the Father. What does this show you about your Heavenly Father?

What's going on in your heart as you realize this?

Write or say a prayer receiving this truth about your Heavenly Father and asking Him to heal the places you've been hurt by father figures in your life.

Day 3

Read Mark 2:1-17

When the men carrying the paralytic couldn't get through, what did they do? (Verse 4)

What does verse 5 say Jesus saw?

How does the story of what the paralytic's friends did speak to your heart about not giving up?

What did Jesus want the scribes to know? (Verse 10)

What was the condition of the paralytic *after* an encounter with Jesus? (Verse 11-12)

Sometimes, faith is simply not giving up when things look like they aren't happening or will never be different. Is there a situation in your life where you've felt like you can't get through? Explain.

Write out a prayer asking Jesus to help you not give up, asking for His direction and for His hand to move in your situation.

Who did Jesus see in verse 14?

Whose house did Jesus dine at? (Verse 15)

What did the scribes and pharisees ask when they saw Jesus dining with tax collectors and sinners?

Write verse 17:

The scribes and Pharisees called out people's sin and condemned them, while Jesus wanted to heal their hearts and lives. What can you observe about your own life situation and coming to Jesus just as you are?

Write out a prayer inviting Jesus to be the physician in your heart and life.

What truth about Jesus stood out to you from this passage?

John 14:9 says when you've seen Jesus, you've seen the Father. What does this show you about your Heavenly Father?

What's going on in your heart as you realize this?

Write or say a prayer receiving this truth about your Heavenly Father and asking Him to heal the places you've been hurt by father figures in your life.

Day 4

Read Mark 2:18-28

Write verse 21:

Often, Jesus will do a new work in us, and as He does, we let go of some of the old ways; old relationships, old patterns, old ways of relating with the world.

Write out a prayer surrendering the old ways in your life and ask the Lord to do a new thing in those areas of your life.

What did Jesus's disciples do that didn't fit the Pharisees' old way of doing things? (Verse 23-24)

In your own words, summarize Jesus' answer to the Pharisees. (Verse 25-28)

What truth about Jesus stood out to you from this passage?

John 14:9 says when you've seen Jesus, you've seen the Father. What does this show you about your Heavenly Father?

What's going on in your heart as you realize this?

Write or say a prayer receiving this truth about your Heavenly Father and asking Him to heal the places you've been hurt by father figures in your life.

Day 5

Read Mark 3:1-19

Who did Jesus meet when He entered the synagogue? (Verse 1)

What direction did Jesus give the man? (Verse 3)

Why was Jesus grieved and angry? (Verse 5)

Jesus directed the man again. What did He tell the man to do?

What was the condition of this man *after* an encounter with Jesus?

Think about one way this man's life must have changed because of his encounter with Jesus.

What did the crowd who had afflictions do? (Verse 10)

And what does this same verse say about the number of people Jesus healed?

What did the unclean spirits do when they saw Jesus? (Verse 11)

Write verse 13:

Who did Jesus call?

Have you struggled with feeling unwanted?

Look up John 6:44. Write it here.

What does this verse say about who drew you to Jesus?

Write John 6:37 here.

What does this verse say about rejection?

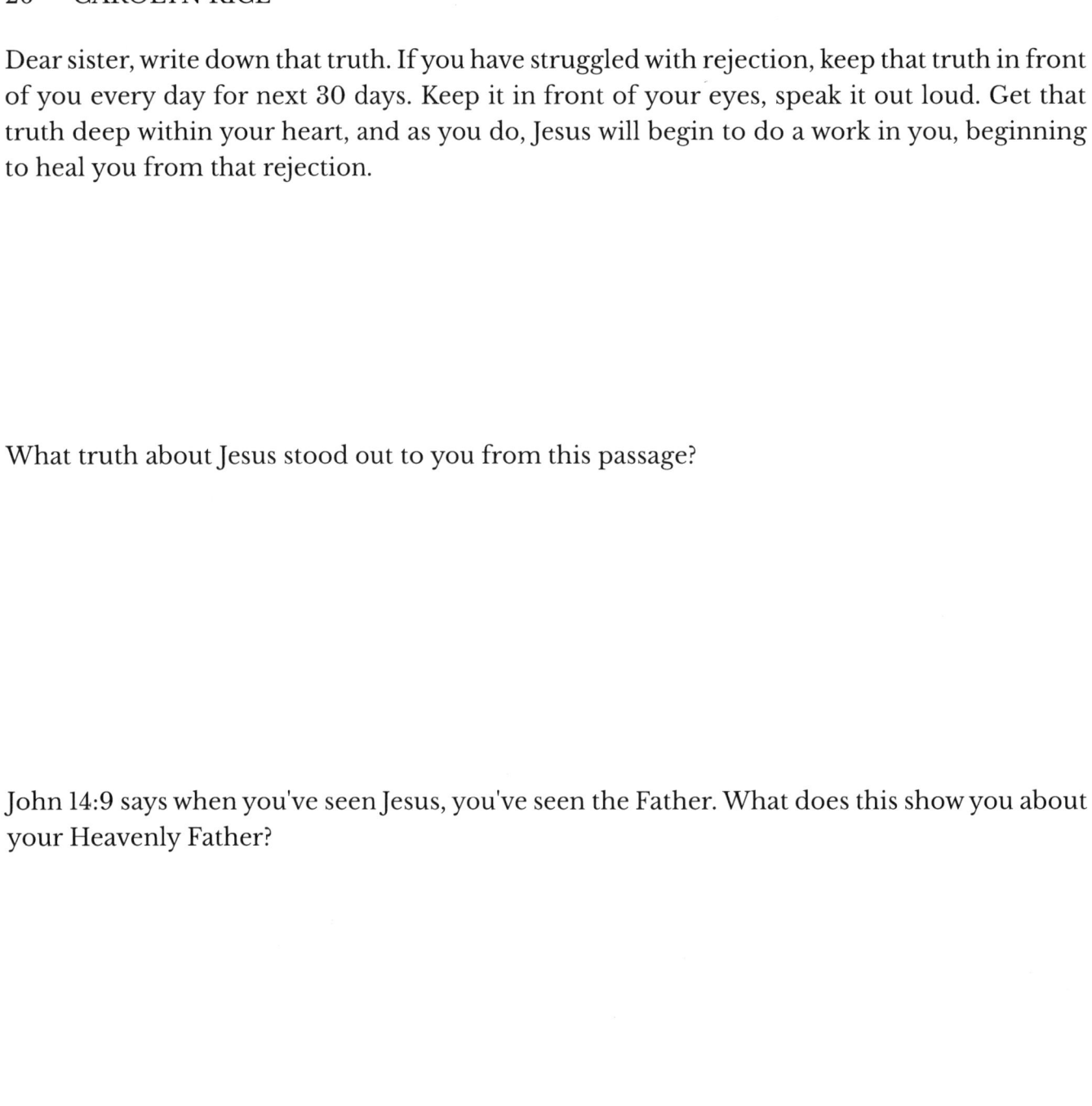

Dear sister, write down that truth. If you have struggled with rejection, keep that truth in front of you every day for next 30 days. Keep it in front of your eyes, speak it out loud. Get that truth deep within your heart, and as you do, Jesus will begin to do a work in you, beginning to heal you from that rejection.

What truth about Jesus stood out to you from this passage?

John 14:9 says when you've seen Jesus, you've seen the Father. What does this show you about your Heavenly Father?

What's going on in your heart as you realize this?

Write or say a prayer receiving this truth about your Heavenly Father and asking Him to heal the places you've been hurt by father figures in your life.

Day 6

Read Mark 3:20-35

What do Jesus' own people say about Him? (Verse 21)

What do the scribes say? (Verse 22)

In your own words, describe what Jesus speaks about this in verse 23-27.

Have you ever struggled with what other people have said about you or how they defined you? Explain.

You can ask God to wipe ungodly words spoken over you away from your heart and bring healing in their place. If you would like, pray this prayer with me:

Father God, I pray that you wipe every ugly word that's been spoken over me away from my heart. I break the power of those words now, in the name of Jesus. I also invite You, Father, to bring healing to those places where my heart was wounded because of those words. I thank You that You hear my prayer, and You will continue this healing work in me as I follow you in everyday life. In Jesus' name, amen.

What truth about Jesus stood out to you from this passage?

John 14:9 says when you've seen Jesus, you've seen the Father. What does this show you about your Heavenly Father?

What's going on in your heart as you realize this?

Write or say a prayer receiving this truth about your Heavenly Father and asking Him to heal the places you've been hurt by father figures in your life.

Day 7

Read Mark 4:1-20

Here we come across Jesus teaching a parable, then explaining this parable to His disciples. Before going any further, let's discuss what a parable is.

In the Greek, parable means "an earthly story with a heavenly meaning." *

Let's take a closer look.

What is the Sower actually sowing? (Verse 14)

What happens to the seed sown by the wayside? (Verse 4)

Now read verse 15 and write in your own words Jesus' explanation of the seed sown on the wayside.

What happened to the seed that fell on stony ground? (Verse 5-6)

Now read verses 16-17 and describe Jesus' explanation of the seed sown on stony ground.

What happened to the seed that fell among thorns? (Verse 7)

Now Read verses 18-19 and write down what the thorns are.

What happened to the seed that was sown on good ground? (Verse 8)

Now read verse 20 and write down what it takes to be good ground for the Word.

Do you recognize anything from this parable that could steal the Word in your own life?

If you do, pray over each one and ask Jesus to make your heart into good ground for the Word. Use the prayer below or write your own prayer:

Father God, I surrender these areas in my life that have been stealing Your Word from taking root in my life. I ask that You gently weed out these things from the garden of my heart and make me into good ground for your Word. I pray Father, that you give me understanding of your Word and how I can apply it to my own life as I read. In Jesus's mighty name, amen.

What truth about Jesus stood out to you from this passage?

John 14:9 says when you've seen Jesus, you've seen the Father. What does this show you about your Heavenly Father?

What's going on in your heart as you realize this?

Write or say a prayer receiving this truth about your Heavenly Father and asking Him to heal the places you've been hurt by father figures in your life.

Day 8

Read Mark 4:21-41

Write verse 22:

What does this promise speak to your heart?

What is the command in verse 24?

What does this verse speak to you about guarding your heart and mind?

Verse 26-29 talks about a seed being planted and how it grows. After yesterday's reading about the seeds being sown, what can you observe about how the Word grows when you plant it in your heart?

When you first plant the seed, does it look like anything is growing?

And when the seed first comes up, does it look grand or beautiful?

When the seed has had time to grow, and continues being watered and nurtured, what does it yield?

What does this parable say about us knowing how the seed grows? (Verse 27)

Look up Ecclesiastes 3:11. Write the first sentence of that verse below.

What does this verse speak to your heart about what God is doing in your life?

Describe the mustard seed in verses 30-32.

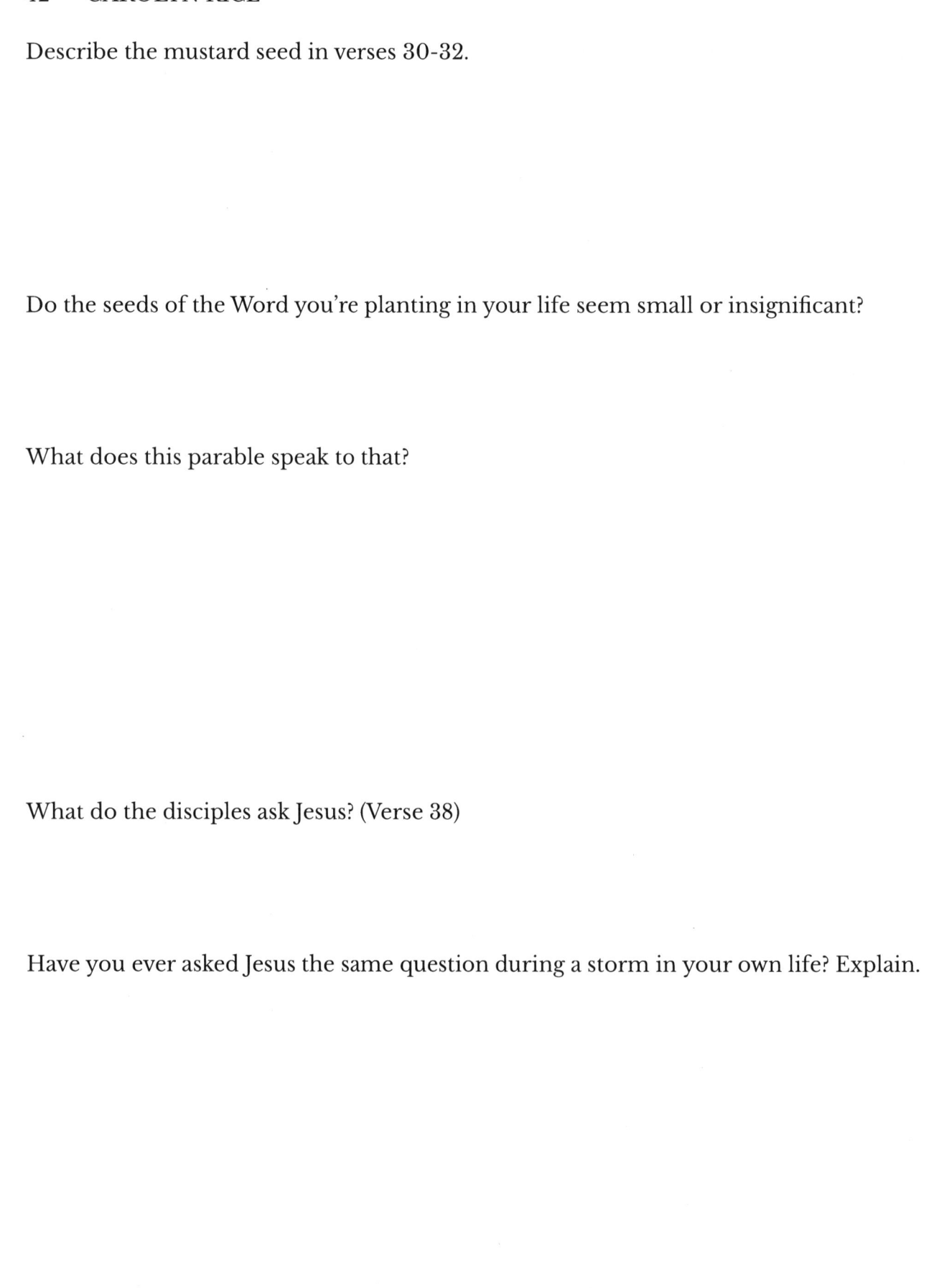

Do the seeds of the Word you're planting in your life seem small or insignificant?

What does this parable speak to that?

What do the disciples ask Jesus? (Verse 38)

Have you ever asked Jesus the same question during a storm in your own life? Explain.

What words did Jesus speak to the storm? (Verse 39)

Describe what happened next. (Verse 40-41)

What can you observe about how God works in your heart and life from this section?

Have you wanted instant growth?

Consider the reading from yesterday about the seeds planted on the wayside, stony ground and among thorns. Then consider how that seed in good ground grows, deeply rooted, and consistently nurtured over time. Quiet your heart and mind for a moment, and then write down anything you feel the Lord is speaking to your heart.

Look again at Ecclesiastes 3:11.

Write out a prayer based on this scripture, asking Your Heavenly Father to help you consistently plant the Word in your life and be ok with growth that takes time. Ask Him to help you know that He's working in your life, even when you can't see anything happening above ground.

What truth about Jesus stood out to you from this passage?

John 14:9 says when you've seen Jesus, you've seen the Father. What does this show you about your Heavenly Father?

What's going on in your heart as you realize this?

Write or say a prayer receiving this truth about your Heavenly Father and asking Him to heal the places you've been hurt by father figures in your life.

Day 9

Read Mark 5:1-20

This chapter starts off with Jesus arriving in the country of the Gadarenes. Immediately, He is met by a man who needed an encounter with Him.

What did this man have? (Verse 2)

Describe this man's dwelling place. (Verse 3)

What happened when people tried to chain him? (Verse 4)

What did this man spend his days doing? (Verse 5)

Based on these verses, there is only one word I can think of that describes what this man was in.

Torment.

What did this man do when he saw Jesus? (Verse 6)

Describe what happened next in your own words. (Verse 8-13)

What was the condition of this man *after* an encounter with Jesus? (Verse 15)

When the man wanted to come with Jesus, what did Jesus tell the man to do? (Verse 19)

In the last part of verse 19, what does your Bible say Jesus had for this man?

After reading how Jesus changed this man's life and what Jesus felt for him, what can you observe about Jesus and what He wants to do in your life?

What truth about Jesus stood out to you from this passage?

John 14:9 says when you've seen Jesus, you've seen the Father. What does this show you about your Heavenly Father?

What's going on in your heart as you realize this?

Write or say a prayer receiving this truth about your Heavenly Father and asking Him to heal the places you've been hurt by father figures in your life.

Day 10

Read Mark 5:21-43

Who was Jairus? (Verse 22)

What did he do when he saw Jesus?

What was Jairus's situation before an encounter with Jesus? (Verse 23)

And what was Jesus' response? (Verse 24)

But before Jesus gets to Jairus's house, there's another encounter.

Describe the condition of this woman who needed an encounter with Jesus. (Verse 25)

How long had she suffered?

What had been her experience with physicians? (Verse 26)

Describe her financial situation.

What does this same verse say about the state of her condition?

What did she do when she heard about Jesus? (Verse 27-28)

When she touched Jesus, what happened? (Verse 29)

Describe Jesus' response to this woman. (Verse 30-34)

All of this happened while Jairus was still waiting for Jesus. Imagine what Jairus must have been feeling, knowing his daughter was at death's door, that Jesus was finally on the way, and then having to wait while Jesus stopped to help someone else.

Soon, people arrived to tell Jairus news about his daughter. What do they tell him? (Verse 35)

And what did they say he shouldn't do?

Jesus heard this and immediately responded. What was Jesus' direction to Jairus? (Verse 36)

Who did Jesus permit to follow Him to the house? (Verse 37)

Why do you think he permitted only them?

Have you ever prayed for Jesus to work in a situation, and watched as someone else got what you prayed for, while it seemed like things got worse for you? Explain.

Did you have people who spoke hopelessness to you during that time?

And did you have people who spoke hope?

In that moment, who did you want around you, the ones who spoke hope, or hopelessness?

What happened when Jesus arrived at Jairus' house? (Verse 38-43)

Who did He put outside?

And who did He let in?

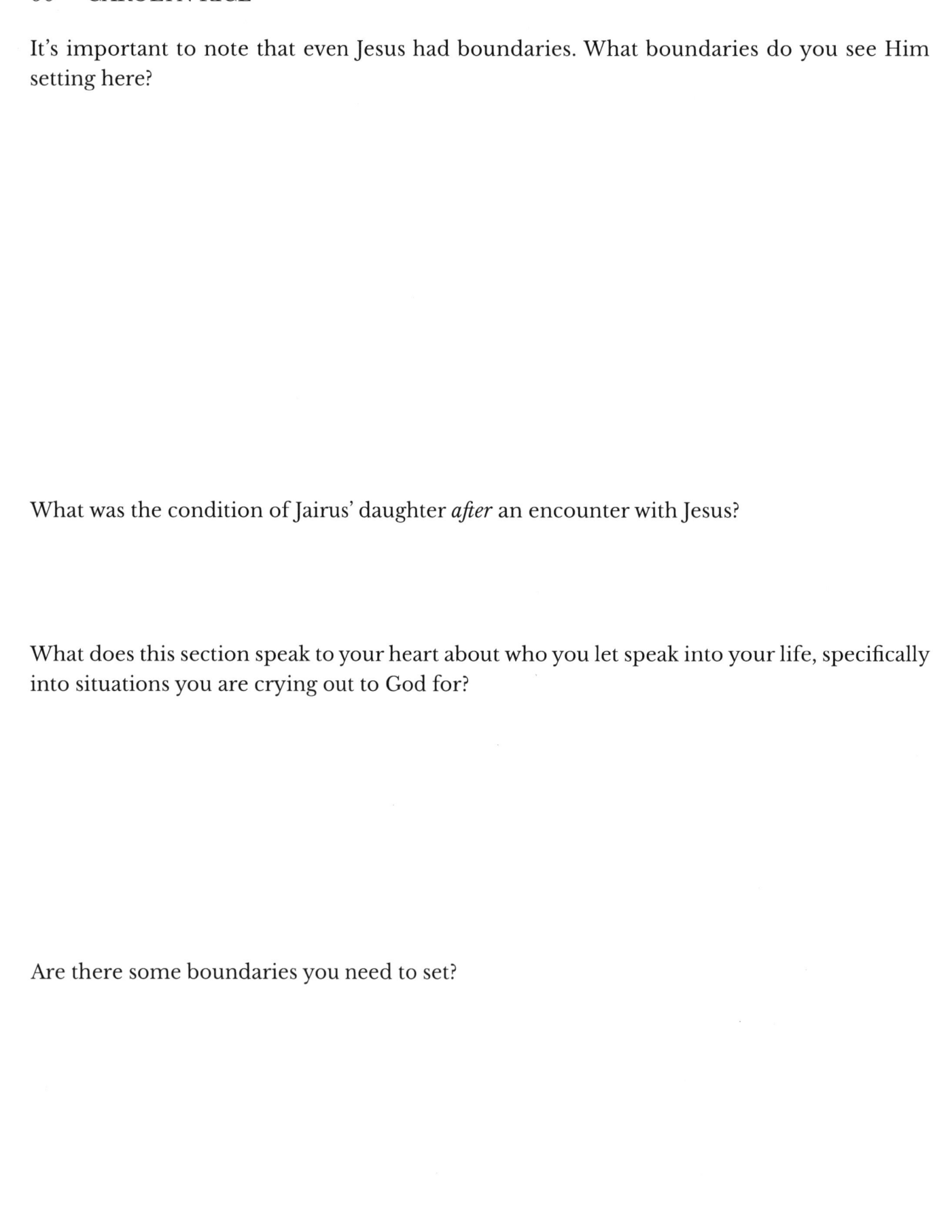

It's important to note that even Jesus had boundaries. What boundaries do you see Him setting here?

What was the condition of Jairus' daughter *after* an encounter with Jesus?

What does this section speak to your heart about who you let speak into your life, specifically into situations you are crying out to God for?

Are there some boundaries you need to set?

What relationships do you want to lean into?

Which ones do you want to let go?

Write out a prayer asking God to put people in your life who will encourage you and speak hope into your heart.

What truth about Jesus stood out to you from this passage?

John 14:9 says when you've seen Jesus, you've seen the Father. What does this show you about your Heavenly Father?

What's going on in your heart as you realize this?

Write or say a prayer receiving this truth about your Heavenly Father and asking Him to heal the places you've been hurt by father figures in your life.

Day 11

Read Mark 6:1-29

Where did Jesus arrive? (Verse 1)

Why were the people offended at Him? (Verse 3)

Write verse 6:4 here.

Why do you think this is?

What could Jesus not do in His own country? (Verse 5)

What did He marvel at? (Verse 6)

In these first few verses, there are two things that describe the people in His own country. What were they?

    1. (   )Verse 3

    2. (   )Verse 6

What condition did Jesus have to leave these people in?

What can you observe about the difference between His own countrymen and the people Jesus has healed so far in the book of Mark?

What was Jesus' command to His disciples about someone who would not receive or hear them? (Verse 11)

Look up Matthew 18:15-17

What are you to do first if someone sins against you?

And if they won't hear you, what do you do next?

What happens if they still refuse to hear you?

Read Mark 6:11 again.

How can you apply this to your own life when someone rejects you and will not hear you?

Describe what happened to John the Baptist. (Verse 14-29)

What did Herodias hold against John? (Verse 18-19)

How did Herod feel about John? (Verse 20)

Yet Herodias manipulated Herod into beheading John. What did she do? (Verse 21-24)

From this section, what can you observe about offense?

If you have places in your life where you've been holding onto offense, I invite you to pray the following prayer:

Father God, I lift the offense I hold against (　　　) into Your hands. I lift up to You the hurt I experienced at (　　　)'s hands. I choose now to forgive (　　　) and surrender her/him to You. (　　) is Your burden and not mine. Thank you, Jesus, that I can still have boundaries and not allow (　　　) to hurt me anymore. I ask that you heal me from every wound (　　　) caused in my life, and I ask for Your help to remove every bitter root of offense from my heart. I thank You that You will continue to work in me over time, and that You hear my prayer of surrender. In Jesus' name I pray, amen.

What truth about Jesus stood out to you from this passage?

John 14:9 says when you've seen Jesus, you've seen the Father. What does this show you about your Heavenly Father?

What's going on in your heart as you realize this?

Write or say a prayer receiving this truth about your Heavenly Father and asking Him to heal the places you've been hurt by father figures in your life.

Day 12

Read Mark 6:30-56

What did Jesus tell His disciples to do after a time of ministry? (Verse 31)

Do you take time to rest after you've given your time and energy to others?

Why or why not?

Where in your life can you set some boundaries or do some pruning, so you have that time to rest?

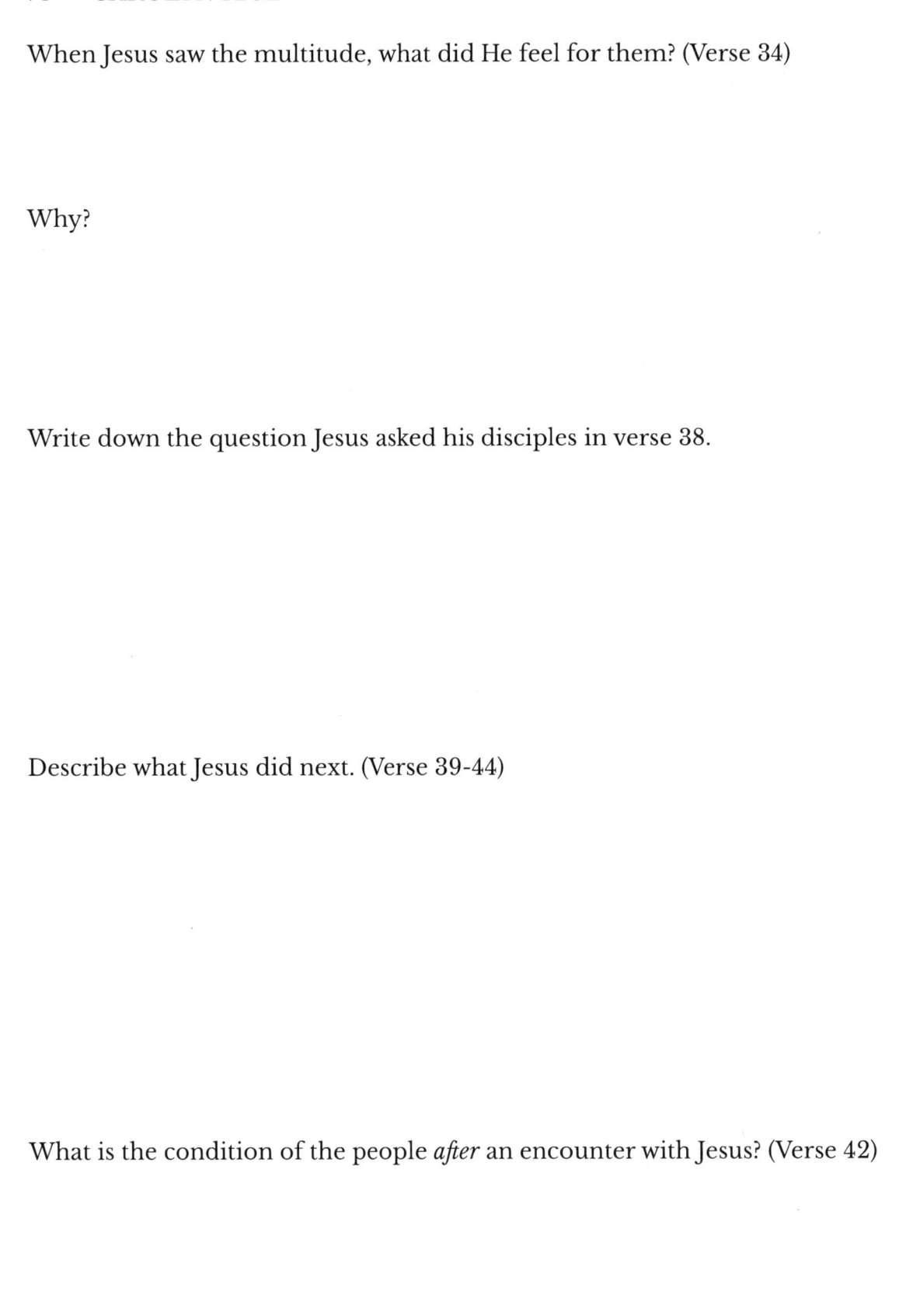

When Jesus saw the multitude, what did He feel for them? (Verse 34)

Why?

Write down the question Jesus asked his disciples in verse 38.

Describe what Jesus did next. (Verse 39-44)

What is the condition of the people *after* an encounter with Jesus? (Verse 42)

Has Jesus asked you to do or give something you feel is insignificant?

What does this section speak to your heart about what God does with the things we do or give to Him, no matter how small?

Where does Jesus send His disciples next? (Verse 45)

What did Jesus see His disciples were doing? (Verse 48)

What was against them?

Have you ever felt like God sent you into a situation, or led you to do something, and suddenly everything was against you? Explain.

What happened when Jesus got into the boat with the disciples? (Verse 51)

Dear Sister, sometimes we don't understand what God is doing in the moment, but if you ask Jesus into the boat with you, He will carry you through those hard times. And if you continue following His leading and guidance, refusing to give up or give in to discouragement, one day you will reap a harvest.

There are a couple of verses that have carried me through times like this.

Write Galatians 6:9 here.

Write Proverbs 3:5-6 here.

Write out a prayer asking Jesus to get into the boat with you, whatever situation you are in. Ask Him to help you trust Him, to not give up or lean on your own understanding, and to direct your steps.

What happened when Jesus came to the land of Gennesaret? (Verse 53-56)

What was the condition of those who begged that they might touch His robe? (Verse 56)

And what was the condition of those who touched Him? (Verse 56)

What do you think their lives were like *after* that encounter with Jesus?

What truth about Jesus stood out to you from this passage?

John 14:9 says when you've seen Jesus, you've seen the Father. What does this show you about your Heavenly Father?

What's going on in your heart as you realize this?

Write or say a prayer receiving this truth about your Heavenly Father and asking Him to heal the places you've been hurt by father figures in your life.

Day 13

Read Mark 7:1-23

What were the Pharisees concerned about? (Verse 2)

Why? (Verse 3-4)

What did they ask Jesus? (Verse 5)

When Jesus answered, what did He say about their hearts? (Verse 6-7)

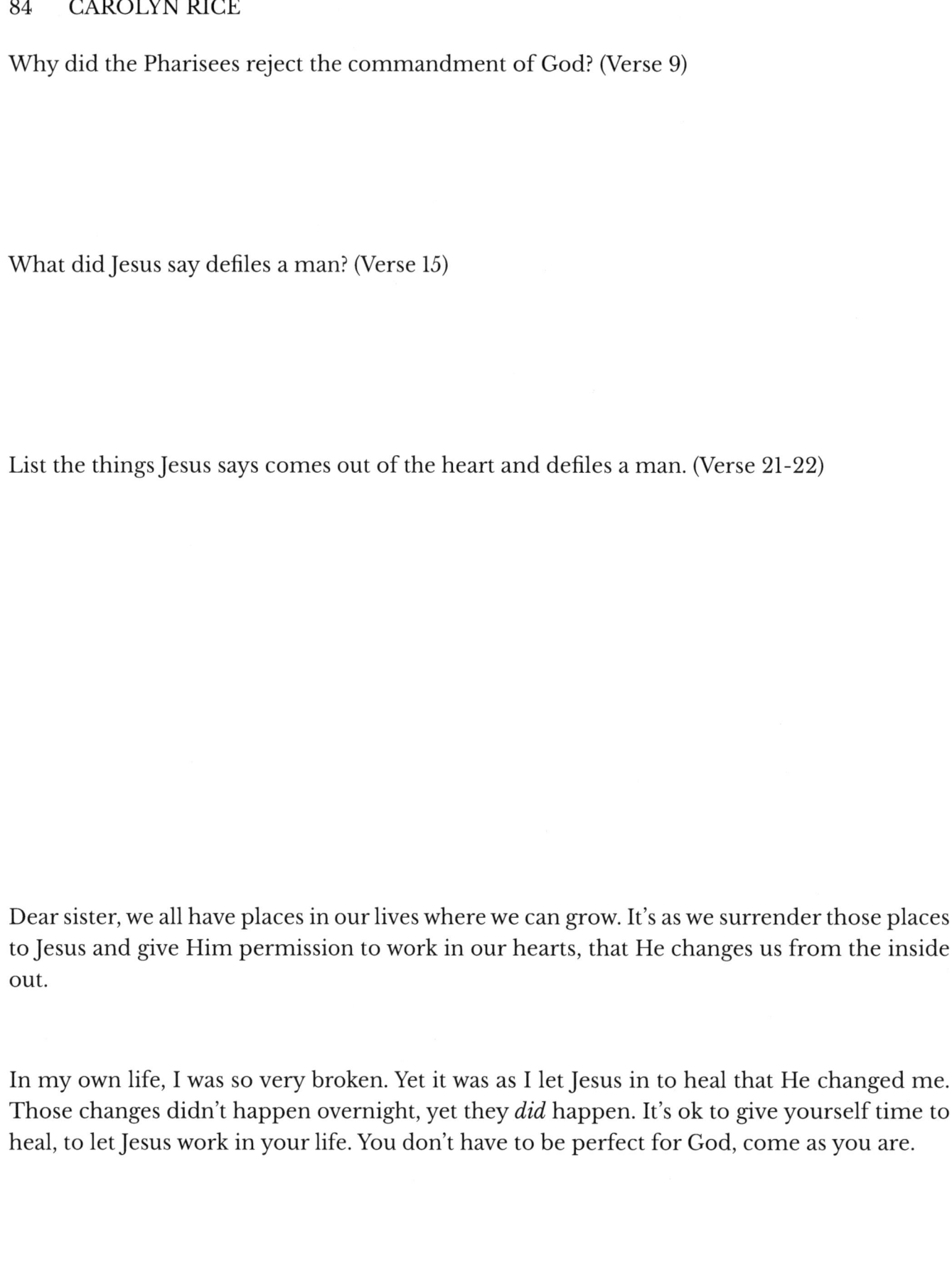

Why did the Pharisees reject the commandment of God? (Verse 9)

What did Jesus say defiles a man? (Verse 15)

List the things Jesus says comes out of the heart and defiles a man. (Verse 21-22)

Dear sister, we all have places in our lives where we can grow. It's as we surrender those places to Jesus and give Him permission to work in our hearts, that He changes us from the inside out.

In my own life, I was so very broken. Yet it was as I let Jesus in to heal that He changed me. Those changes didn't happen overnight, yet they *did* happen. It's ok to give yourself time to heal, to let Jesus work in your life. You don't have to be perfect for God, come as you are.

Look up 1 Samuel 16:7

What does this verse say man looks at?

But what does it say God looks at?

No matter how other people have treated you, judged you, or defined you, they are looking through the lenses of their own hearts.

God sees your heart, dear sister. He sees every desire and every longing for healing. He's heard every prayer, and He has a plan for your healing.

Do you want to give God permission to work in your heart? If so, write out a prayer giving Him that permission.

What truth about Jesus stood out to you from this passage?

John 14:9 says when you've seen Jesus, you've seen the Father. What does this show you about your Heavenly Father?

What's going on in your heart as you realize this?

Write or say a prayer receiving this truth about your Heavenly Father and asking Him to heal the places you've been hurt by father figures in your life.

Day 14

Read Mark 7:24-37

What was the condition of the woman's daughter in verse 25?

When this woman encountered Jesus, what did she do?

Who was she? (Verse 26)

What was Jesus' initial answer? (Verse 27)

Note that Jesus was first sent to the lost sheep of Israel (See Matthew 15:24). It was only later, after Jesus' ascension, that the Holy Spirit spoke to Peter about going to the gentiles (See Acts 10). A gentile is a person who is not Jewish. So, at this point in history, this woman was outside the people Jesus was called to go to. Remember that the gentiles have been grafted in (See Romans 11). So, there is not one who is a little dog in the Kingdom any longer.

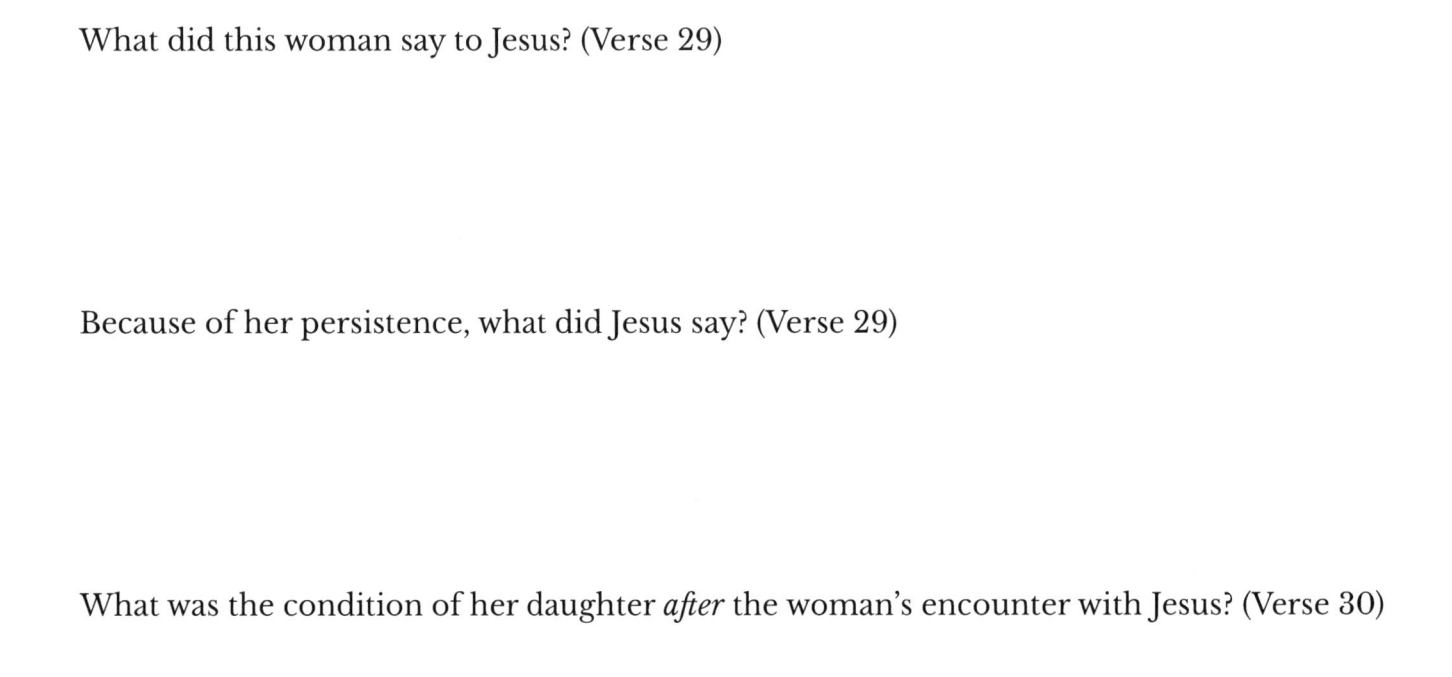

What did this woman say to Jesus? (Verse 29)

Because of her persistence, what did Jesus say? (Verse 29)

What was the condition of her daughter *after* the woman's encounter with Jesus? (Verse 30)

Have you ever felt like you were unworthy, or somehow on the outside? Explain.

Write John 1:12. here.

Who does this say you are again?

Dear sister, you are not outside of the Kingdom if you have accepted Christ as your Lord and Savior. If you have not accepted Christ, there is a prayer in the back of this book that will help you do that.

Look up Deuteronomy 32:10.

What does this verse say God's people are?

Are you one of God's daughters? (See again John 1:12)

So, what does this say about you?

Look up Isaiah 49:16.

Whose name is written on the palm of God's hand?

So where is your name written?

Write Psalm 139:17 here.

What does this say about how much God thinks about you?

Today, I would like to do something different. If you have struggled with the belief that God does not hear you, or you are on the outside, I want to pray with you, inviting Jesus to break that lie off your heart and mind.

Prayer

In the name of Jesus, I break the power of the lie that said I was not good enough, or that I was on the outside of God's mercy and grace, that I didn't belong in His kingdom. I renounce every agreement I've made with that lie, and I command it to fall to the ground now, having no more power over my mind, heart, or life. Jesus, I invite you to come into the garden of my heart and wipe out the lies that have taken root there. Show me who I am in You, and that You are for me, not against me. Help me grow in the knowledge of Your great love for me, and the knowledge of who I am in You, a daughter of the King of all Kings. Help me know and stand in the authority that the devil has no more right to my life. In Jesus' mighty name, I pray, amen.

What truth about Jesus stood out to you from this passage?

John 14:9 says when you've seen Jesus, you've seen the Father. What does this show you about your Heavenly Father?

What's going on in your heart as you realize this?

Write or say a prayer receiving this truth about your Heavenly Father and asking Him to heal the places you've been hurt by father figures in your life.

Day 15

Read Mark 8:1-21

What did Jesus feel toward the multitude? (Verse 2)

When the disciples questioned Him, what did Jesus ask them? (Verse 5)

In your own words, describe what happened next. (Verse 6-10)

How many loaves were there? (Verse 5)

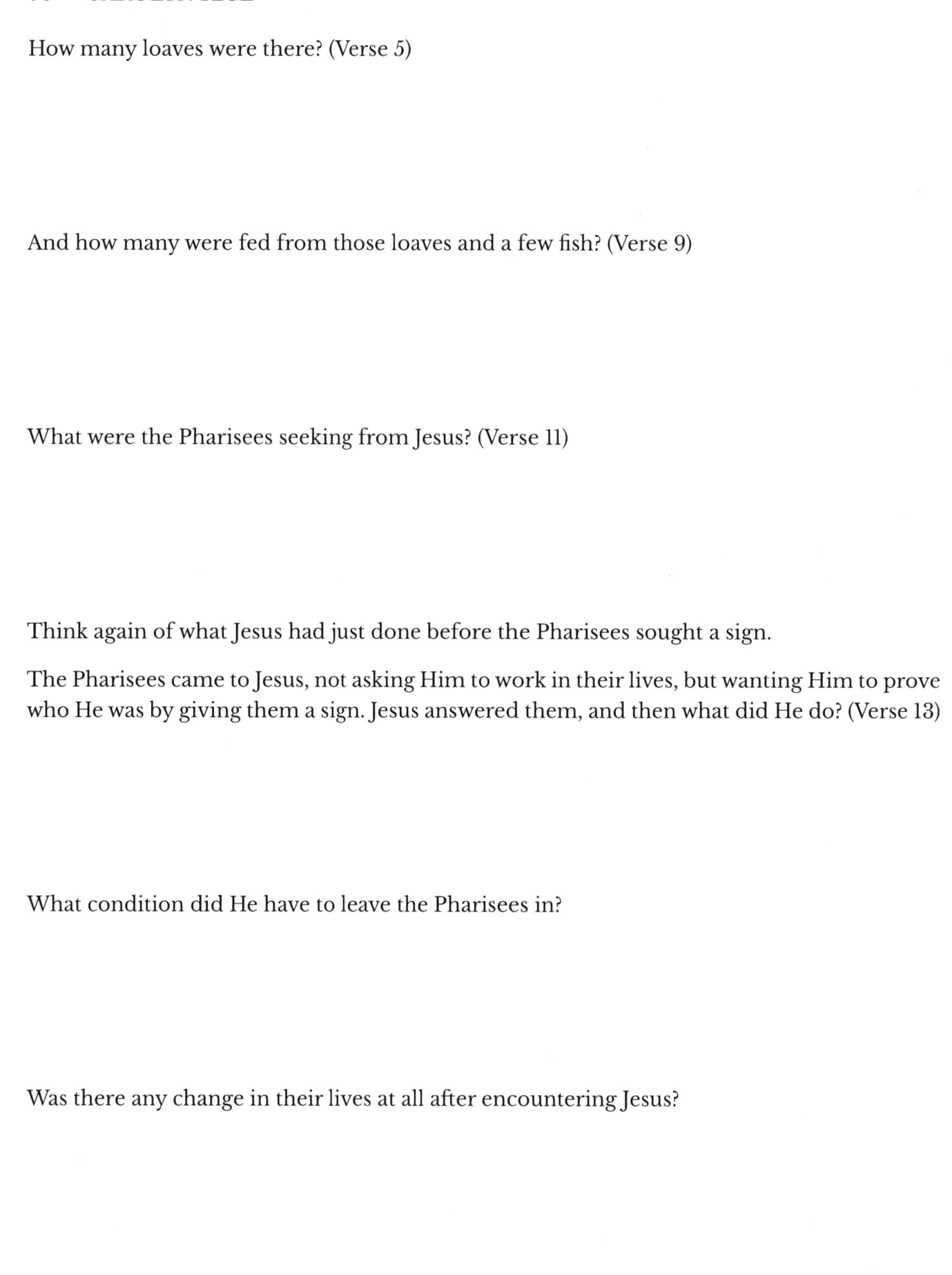

And how many were fed from those loaves and a few fish? (Verse 9)

What were the Pharisees seeking from Jesus? (Verse 11)

Think again of what Jesus had just done before the Pharisees sought a sign.

The Pharisees came to Jesus, not asking Him to work in their lives, but wanting Him to prove who He was by giving them a sign. Jesus answered them, and then what did He do? (Verse 13)

What condition did He have to leave the Pharisees in?

Was there any change in their lives at all after encountering Jesus?

Why do you think that was?

What did Jesus warn the disciples about? (Verse 15)

What did the disciples reason His warning was about? (Verse 16)

When Jesus became aware of their reasoning, what did He remind them of? (Verse 17-21)

Think back upon your life and list a few of the things God has done for you.

(Hint: one of them could be your salvation.)

Write out a prayer thanking your Heavenly Father for working in your life.

Now, write down something you are waiting on God for.

How does remembering what He's already done affect how you look at this situation?

Dear sister, whenever you encounter a problem, always recall what God has already done in your life. Thank Him and praise Him for those things. Thank Him for His promises and that He is the same, yesterday, today, and forever (See Hebrews 13:8). Then, come to Him regarding this new situation on your heart.

What truth about Jesus stood out to you from this passage?

John 14:9 says when you've seen Jesus, you've seen the Father. What does this show you about your Heavenly Father?

What's going on in your heart as you realize this?

Write or say a prayer receiving this truth about your Heavenly Father and asking Him to heal the places you've been hurt by father figures in your life.

Day 16

Read Mark 8:22-38

Who did they bring to Jesus in Bethsaida? (Verse 22)

How many times did Jesus put His hands on the man's eyes? (Verse 23-25)

What was the condition of this man *after* an encounter with Jesus? (Verse 25)

Is there an area in your life where Jesus has touched but isn't fully healed yet?

Write Philippians 1:6 here.

Dear sister, just because it's not done right away doesn't mean God has forgotten or that He's done working. Keep moving forward, knowing that the Lord is still working in your life.

What did Jesus ask His disciples? (Verse 27)

If Jesus asked you this question, what would you say?

What did Jesus say to Peter when Peter rebuked Jesus? (Verse 33)

Let's look at this verse in some different translations.

For you are not mindful of the things of God, but the things of men." ~ NKJV

"You are seeing things merely from a human point of view, not from God's." ~ NLT

"You do not have in mind the concerns of God, but merely human concerns." ~ NIV

For you are not setting your mind on the things of God, but on the things of man." ~ ESV

Notice the ESV's wording. **Setting Your Mind.**

There is another verse in the Bible that talks about setting your mind.

Write Colossians 3:2 here.

Following is a list of ways we can set our mind on God and His Word. Circle one way you will set your mind on the things of God this week.

> Pray His Word back to Him
>
> Memorize His Word
>
> Journal about His Word
>
> Think about the Word
>
> Talk about the Word

When will you do this?

What truth about Jesus stood out to you from this passage?

John 14:9 says when you've seen Jesus, you've seen the Father. What does this show you about your Heavenly Father?

What's going on in your heart as you realize this?

Write or say a prayer receiving this truth about your Heavenly Father and asking Him to heal the places you've been hurt by father figures in your life.

Day 17

Read Mark 9:1-29

Describe how Jesus looked when He was transfigured. (Verse 3)

Who appeared with Jesus, and what were they doing? (Verse 4)

What did the voice from the cloud say who Jesus is? (Verse 7)

And what was the voice's command?

In your own words, describe Jesus' answer to the question about Elijah coming first. (Verse 12-13)

Read Matthew 11:11-14

After reading this passage, who would you say is the Elijah Jesus is talking about?

Describe the condition of the son who was brought to the disciples. (Verse 17-18, and 21-22)

What was Jesus' direction? (Verse 19)

What happened when the boy saw Jesus? (Verse 20)

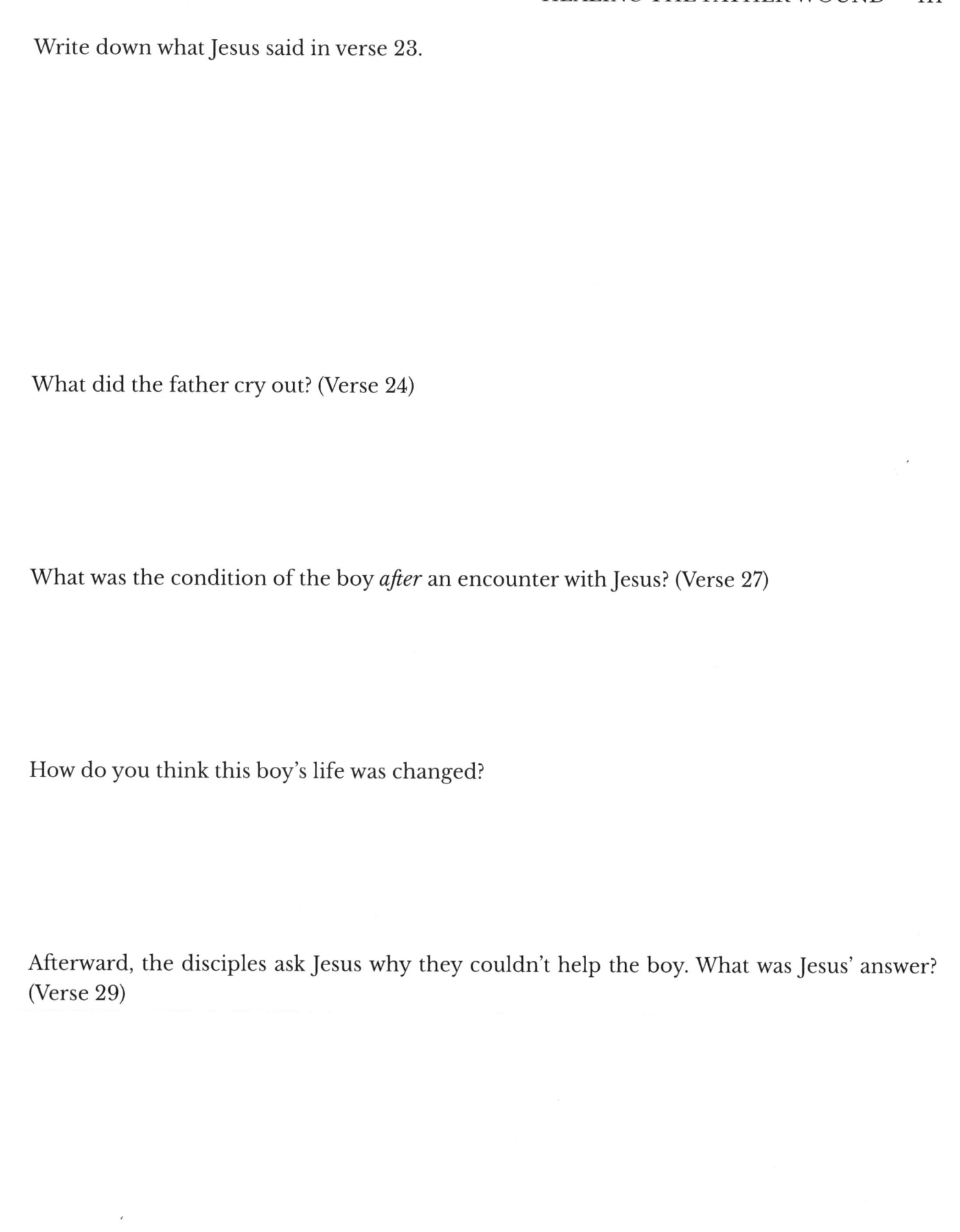

Write down what Jesus said in verse 23.

What did the father cry out? (Verse 24)

What was the condition of the boy *after* an encounter with Jesus? (Verse 27)

How do you think this boy's life was changed?

Afterward, the disciples ask Jesus why they couldn't help the boy. What was Jesus' answer? (Verse 29)

What truth about Jesus stood out to you from this passage?

John 14:9 says when you've seen Jesus, you've seen the Father. What does this show you about your Heavenly Father?

What's going on in your heart as you realize this?

Write or say a prayer receiving this truth about your Heavenly Father and asking Him to heal the places you've been hurt by father figures in your life.

Day 18

Read Mark 9:30-50

What did Jesus tell His disciples? (Verse 31)

What were the disciples disputing about? (Verse 34)

Describe what Jesus said about being the greatest. (Verse 35)

Reflect for a moment on what Jesus told His disciples in verse 31, and what He said about being the greatest in Verse 35. From what you've read about Jesus' life so far, how have you seen Him model greatness?

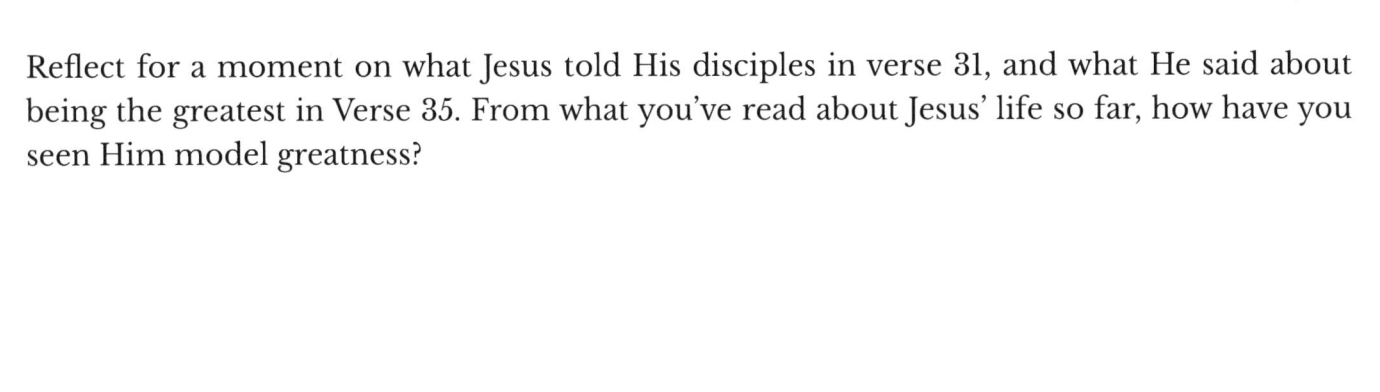

Read verse 36, slowly.

Picture yourself as that little child in your mind. Stay here a moment, and picture yourself sitting in Jesus's arms. What does Jesus speak to your heart?

Now read verse 37.

What does this verse speak to you about anyone who has rejected you?

Write verse 40 here.

In verse 41, what is the promise?

How does verse 42 say Jesus feels about those who cause those who believe in Him to stumble?

Many find verses 43-48 hard to interpret and understand. When that happens, it's good to let the Bible interpret the Bible. A way that you can do this is by looking up cross references, which are other verses that elaborate on the verse you are reading. You can usually find cross references in the footnotes of your Bible or on a site like blueletterbible.org.

Look up the following cross references to verses 43-48 and jot down some notes on what stands out to you.

1 Corinthians 9:27

Galatians 5:24

Psalm 34:14

John 13:34-5

John 15:17-18

Romans 12:18

Galatians 5:14-15

Galatians 5:22

What does verse 49 speak about?

To better understand this verse, we can look at it in some other translations.

For everyone will be seasoned with fire and every sacrifice will be seasoned with salt. ~ NKJV

For everyone will be tested with fire. ~ NLT

Everyone will be salted with fire. ~NIV

In your own words, describe what verse 50 says.

Look up Matthew 5:13. What does this verse say you are?

What truth about Jesus stood out to you from this passage?

John 14:9 says when you've seen Jesus, you've seen the Father. What does this show you about your Heavenly Father?

What's going on in your heart as you realize this?

Write or say a prayer receiving this truth about your Heavenly Father and asking Him to heal the places you've been hurt by father figures in your life.

Day 19

Read Mark 10:1-31

What was the Pharisee's agenda when they asked their question of Jesus? (Verse 2)

The Pharisees were quick to recite the law and what Moses said. Yet, they came to the Son of God with their own agenda. Jesus told them why Moses wrote them that law.

What is the reason?

Why did the people bring the children to Jesus? (Verse 13)

When the disciples rebuked this, how did Jesus feel about it? (Verse 14)

Describe what Jesus says about children and how we as adults should come to Him. (Verse 14-16)

What does it mean to you to come to Jesus as a little child?

What did the rich young ruler ask Jesus? (Verse 17)

After Jesus tells him the commandments to keep, what did the rich young ruler say? (Verse 20)

What was still lacking in the man's life? (Verse 21)

HEALING THE FATHER WOUND 125

In the very last part of this same verse, what did Jesus say the man should do?

This rich young ruler had an encounter with Jesus, the one who could have changed his life in so many ways. Yet he chose to hang onto something else instead of following Jesus.

What was the condition of this man *after* his encounter with Jesus? (Verse 22)

This man knew all the rules and kept them. But Jesus didn't truly have his heart.

What does Jesus say to His disciples after talking with the rich young ruler? (Verse 23-26)

Yet there is still hope. Write verse 27 here.

When I was living in a place of brokenness because of the abuse I had suffered, I often ran to people, or relationships, to try and fill the empty places within me. But God in His mercy showed me I only needed to run to Him, and He would fill those empty places. As I ran to Him above anyone else, He began that healing work in me.

Have you been in that place of trusting things, people, or relationships more than trusting God?

If so, you can pray and tell God you want Him to have your whole heart. Pray the example below or write out your own.

Father God, I have let things or people come in between You and me. I have trusted in things that will someday fall away, that look secure but are not. Father, I want to trust You, to follow You, and to give You my whole heart. I ask You to help me trust You more than I trust in anything or anyone else. In Jesus' name, amen.

Write what Peter says in verse 28.

Have you left any of the people or things listed in verse 29 to follow Jesus?

If so, what is God's promise to you? (Verse 29-30)

Write verse 31 here.

What truth about Jesus stood out to you from this passage?

John 14:9 says when you've seen Jesus, you've seen the Father. What does this show you about your Heavenly Father?

What's going on in your heart as you realize this?

Write or say a prayer receiving this truth about your Heavenly Father and asking Him to heal the places you've been hurt by father figures in your life.

Day 20

Read Mark 10:32-52

What did Jesus tell His disciples would happen to Him? (Verse 33-34)

What is it that James and John wanted from Jesus? (Verse 37)

What question did Jesus answer with? (Verse 38)

Describe what He tells them in verse 39.

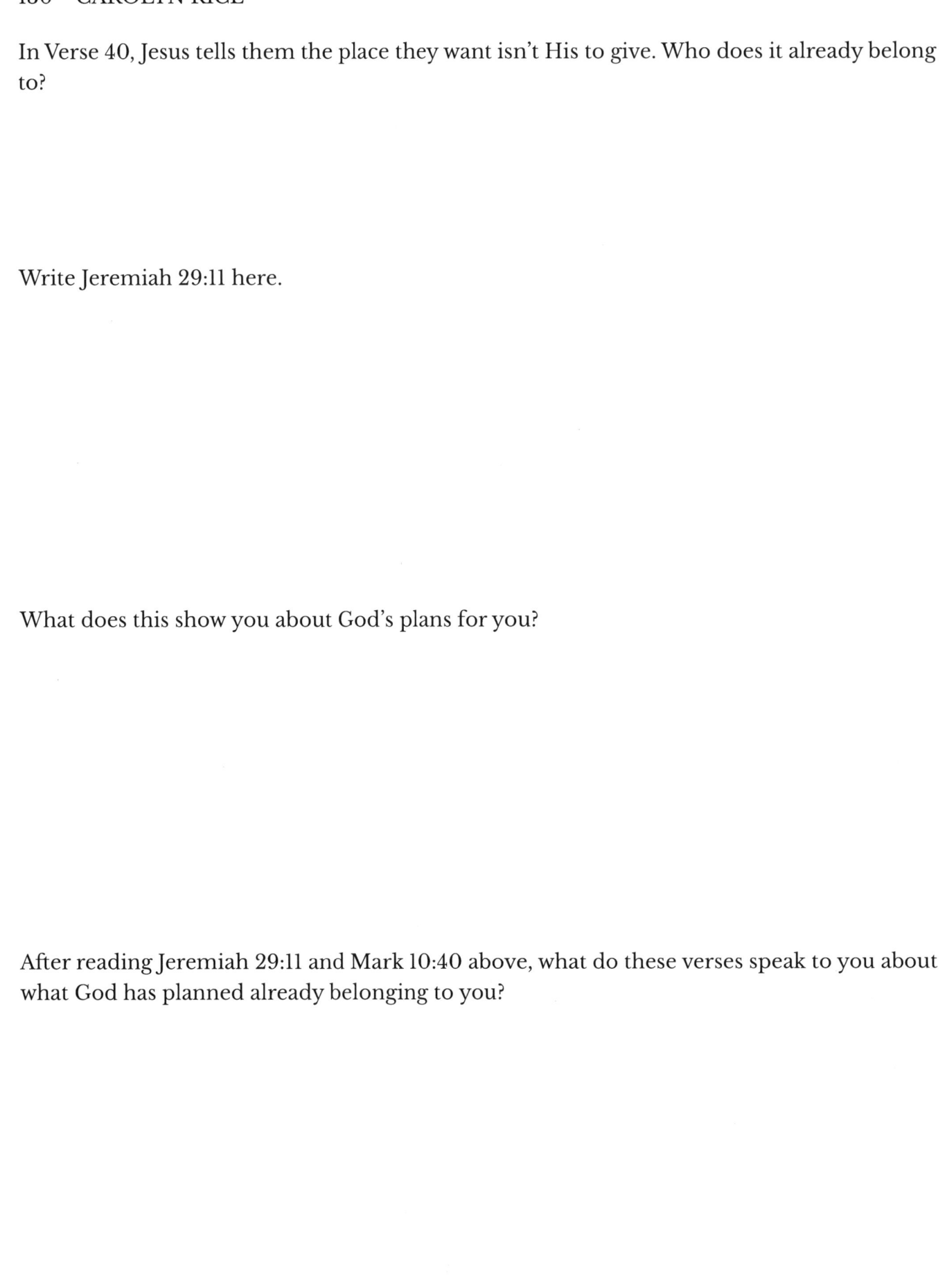

In Verse 40, Jesus tells them the place they want isn't His to give. Who does it already belong to?

Write Jeremiah 29:11 here.

What does this show you about God's plans for you?

After reading Jeremiah 29:11 and Mark 10:40 above, what do these verses speak to you about what God has planned already belonging to you?

Have you felt like you had to strive for what God has for you, to get it yourself instead of simply letting Jesus lead you there?

Do you feel like you've been waiting a long time and you're wondering if God has forgotten you?

If so, I invite you to pray this prayer:

Father God, I ask your forgiveness for striving toward the plan You have for me, instead of simply resting in Your ability to take me there. I want Your Holy Spirit to lead and guide me, instead of being led by fear, insecurity, or any other emotion. Encourage me in the waiting and help me know that I will come into Your plans simply by following You. In Jesus' name, amen.

Jesus explains what greatness is among His followers. What does He say it takes to be great? (Verse 43-45)

What did blind Bartimaeus do when He heard Jesus was coming? (Verse 47)

And what did he do when the people told him to be quiet? (Verse 48)

When Jesus heard Bartimaeus, what was His response? (Verse 49)

Bartimaeus threw something off before he rose and came to Jesus. What was it? (Verse 50)

Describe what happened in verses 51-52.

What was the condition of Bartimaeus *after* an encounter with Jesus?

And what did He do after he received his sight? (Verse 52)

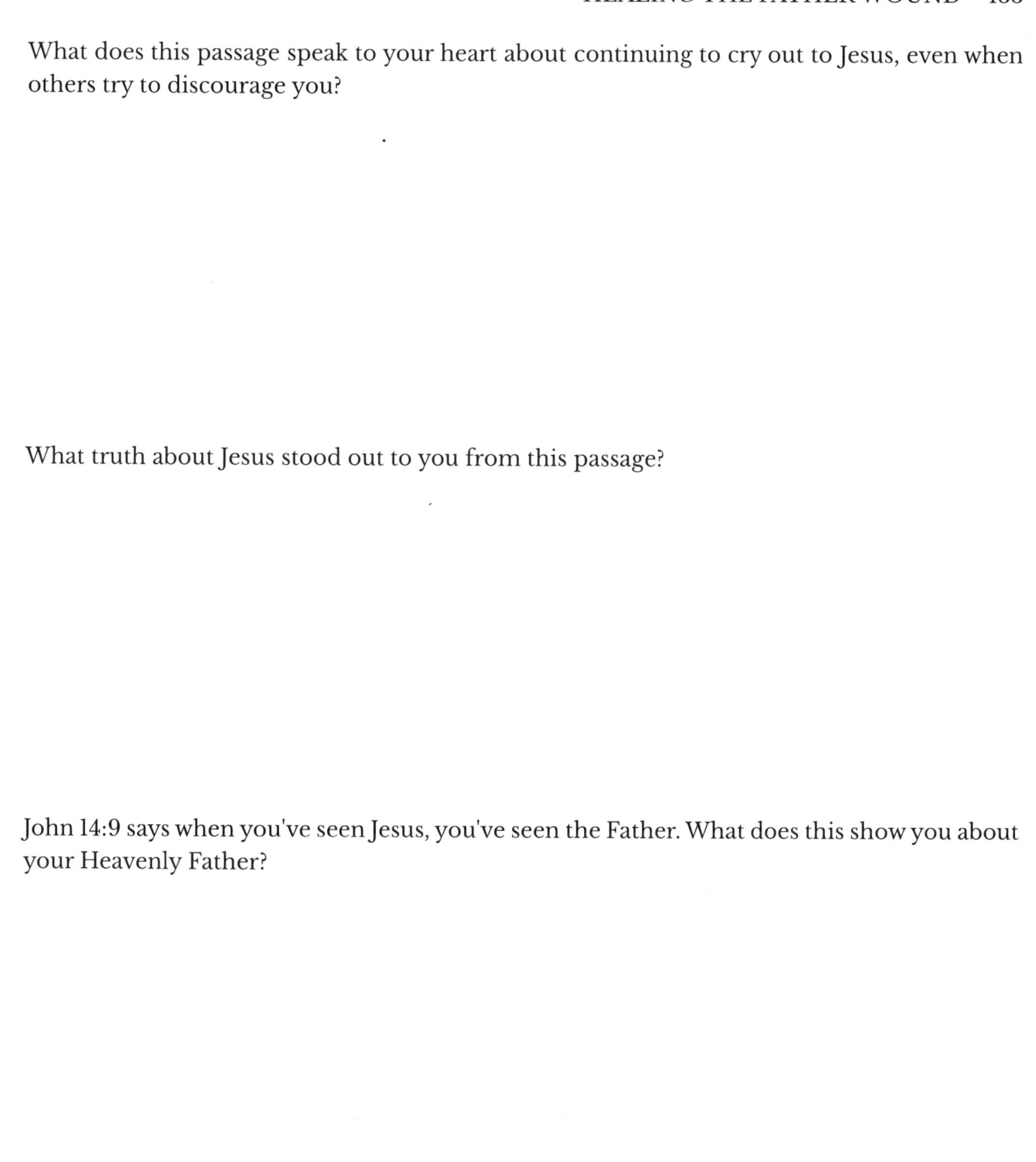

What does this passage speak to your heart about continuing to cry out to Jesus, even when others try to discourage you?

What truth about Jesus stood out to you from this passage?

John 14:9 says when you've seen Jesus, you've seen the Father. What does this show you about your Heavenly Father?

What's going on in your heart as you realize this?

Write or say a prayer receiving this truth about your Heavenly Father and asking Him to heal the places you've been hurt by father figures in your life.

Day 21

Read Mark 11:1-19

Describe what Jesus sent two of his disciples to do. (Verse 2)

What did He tell them to say if someone asked what they were doing? (Verse 3)

The disciples did what Jesus said, and as they were untying the colt, what happened? (Verse 5)

How does this match up with the direction Jesus gave them?

Have you ever felt like you've followed Jesus but ran into situations that discouraged you? Explain.

From this passage, what can you observe about Jesus already knowing about these things?

Read Exodus 13:17-18

When you follow Jesus, there will be battles. There will be times of waiting and wondering why things are taking so long. The enemy of your soul would like nothing better than to stop you from moving forward, discourage you, or hinder your journey with Christ.

But Jesus knows the way to His plans for you. He knows you may experience discouragement, persecution, or suffering. And He has promised to lead you, guide you, and never leave you as an orphan in this life.

Whatever you go through, you are not alone. He is with you, and He knows the way to the other side of what you're going through.

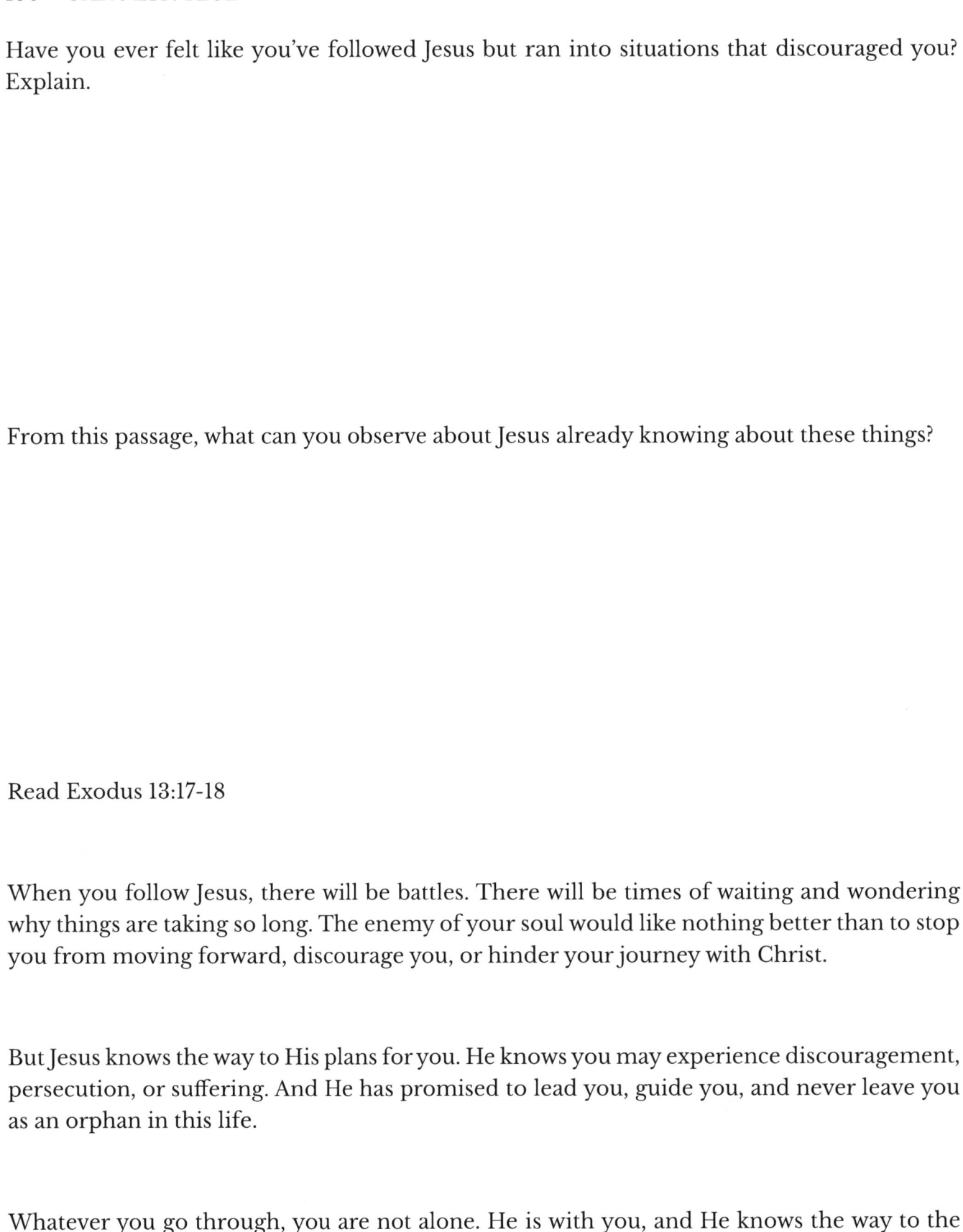

Following are some verses that may encourage you on your journey. Look them up and make a note of the ones that especially speak to your heart.

Isaiah 30:21

John 16:33

1 John 4:4

Matthew 28:20

John 14:18

When you experience battles in your life, I invite you to sit at Jesus' feet in prayer, give Him your tears, all your feelings and the discouragement this world has thrown at you.

Then, when you have felt your feelings and given Him your tears, allow Him to help you back up, dear sister in Christ. Ask Him for His direction, and keep following Him.

What truth about Jesus stood out to you from this passage?

John 14:9 says when you've seen Jesus, you've seen the Father. What does this show you about your Heavenly Father?

What's going on in your heart as you realize this?

Write or say a prayer receiving this truth about your Heavenly Father and asking Him to heal the places you've been hurt by father figures in your life.

Day 22

Read Mark 11: 12 -19

Describe what happened when Jesus came upon the fig tree. (Verse 12-14)

Look up John 15:1-7

How does this passage say you bear fruit?

Read Galatians 5:22-23.

What is the fruit of the Spirit?

Describe what Jesus does when He comes to the temple and sees those who bought and sold there? (Verse 15-16)

What does He say His house shall be called? (Verse 17)

What is one way you can make prayer a priority in your own life?

We are all a work in progress. As we abide in Jesus through being in His word and prayer, we mature, bearing fruit in our lives for the kingdom of God.

What truth about Jesus stood out to you from this passage?

John 14:9 says when you've seen Jesus, you've seen the Father. What does this show you about your Heavenly Father?

What's going on in your heart as you realize this?

Write or say a prayer receiving this truth about your Heavenly Father and asking Him to heal the places you've been hurt by father figures in your life.

Day 23

Read Mark 11: 20-33

What did the disciples come upon in the morning? (Verse 20)

After remembering what Jesus did the day before, what did Peter say? (Verse 21)

What was Jesus's answer in verse 22?

Write verse 23 here.

What is the promise in verse 24?

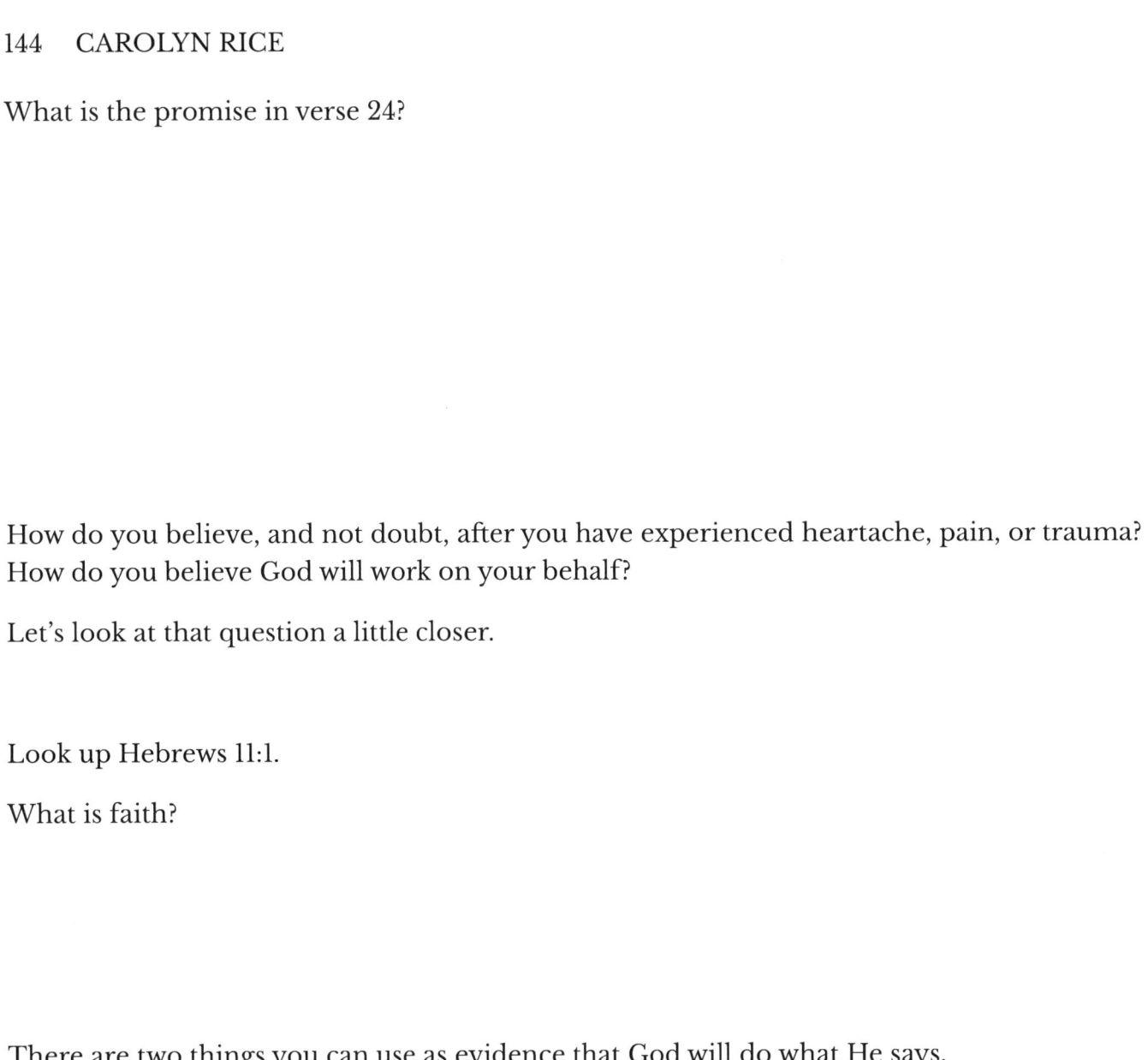

How do you believe, and not doubt, after you have experienced heartache, pain, or trauma? How do you believe God will work on your behalf?

Let's look at that question a little closer.

Look up Hebrews 11:1.

What is faith?

There are two things you can use as evidence that God will do what He says.

The first one is God's Word.

If God has given you a scriptural promise regarding a mountain in your life, write that scripture down where you can see it every day.

If you don't yet have a scripture God has spoken to your heart, ask Him. I invite you to pray the prayer below.

Father God, I ask you to give me a promise that would speak to my heart regarding the situation in my life that has become like a mountain to me. I pray, Father God, for your encouragement and for that truth You give to become real to me. Thank you for showing me the truth of what You say about my situation. In Jesus' name, amen.

The second thing that is evidence God will do what He says is remembering what He has already done in your life. Think for a moment about how God has already answered prayers for you. It could be something small or something big. Write it down.

Write out or say a prayer, thanking God for the promise He's given you and for the ways He has already worked in your life. Tell Him you trust Him to help you overcome this mountain.

What does Jesus say about forgiveness? (Verse 25-26)

After suffering childhood abuse, forgiveness was an enormous struggle for me. I learned to tell the Lord my struggles, and to be brutally honest with Him about my feelings. I also learned I could ask Him for help when I struggled with forgiveness.

If forgiveness has been a struggle for you, I invite you to pray the following prayer with me if you'd like:

Father, I want to obey your command to forgive. Show me what that really means, and that it's ok to have boundaries while walking in forgiveness. Help me grow in implementing healthy boundaries and not allow myself to be hurt again, but to give what was done into Your hands. Bring me to a place of healing. In Jesus' name I pray, amen.

Describe what Jesus did when the chief priests, scribes, and elders questioned His authority? (Verse 27-33)

What truth about Jesus stood out to you from this passage?

John 14:9 says when you've seen Jesus, you've seen the Father. What does this show you about your Heavenly Father?

What's going on in your heart as you realize this?

Write or say a prayer receiving this truth about your Heavenly Father and asking Him to heal the places you've been hurt by father figures in your life.

Day 24

Read Mark 12:1-27

The first verse in chapter 12 tells us that Jesus is teaching by Parables. Remember that a parable is "an earthly story with a heavenly meaning."*

So, as you read the following parable, think about what Heavenly meaning Jesus is illustrating.

The first part talks of a man who planted a vineyard. What else did he do in this very first verse? (Verse 1)

Later, he sent a servant. Why did he send him? (Verse 2)

What did the vinedressers do to this servant? (Verse 3)

The man continued to send servants to the vinedressers. Describe what the vinedressers did to them. (Verse 4-5)

Who did the man send last, and why? (Verse 6)

What did the vinedressers want for themselves?

What did they do to the son? (Verse 8)

What will the owner of the vineyard do? (Verse 9)

In verses 10-11, Jesus references Psalm 118:22. Turn and read that paragraph in Psalm 118 for yourself.

HEALING THE FATHER WOUND   151

We now come out of the parable and see the response of the chief priests, scribes, and elders. What did they seek to do to Jesus? (Verse 12)

Why?

Why didn't they do it?

What spiritual truth do you think Jesus was illustrating in this parable?

After the chief Priests, scribes and elders went away, who did they send? (Verse 13)

Why did they send them?

What did the Pharisees say they knew about Jesus? (Verse 15)

And what was their question?

What was Jesus' question to them?

And His answer? (Verse 16-17)

Right after this, some Sadducees came to question Him as well. Summarize what they ask in your own words. (Verse 19-23)

Jesus spoke of two things they didn't know. What were they? (Verse 24)

What was Jesus' answer to them? (Verse 25-26)

What truth about Jesus stood out to you from this passage?

John 14:9 says when you've seen Jesus, you've seen the Father. What does this show you about your Heavenly Father?

What's going on in your heart as you realize this?

Write or say a prayer receiving this truth about your Heavenly Father and asking Him to heal the places you've been hurt by father figures in your life.

Day 25

Read Mark 12:28-44

What did the Scribe ask Jesus? (Verse 28)

Write verse 30 here.

Write the second commandment Jesus refers to in verse 31.

What did the scribe say all these commandments were more than? (Verse 33)

From this passage, what can you observe about what God wants from you the most?

Write Jesus' response to the scribe. (Verse 34)

How does Jesus question the scribe's teaching? (Verse 35-37)

Jesus was questioning those who thought they knew it all. Can you imagine them trying to wrap their minds around what He'd just asked?

Yet who heard Him gladly? (Verse 37)

HEALING THE FATHER WOUND   157

In the next few verses, Jesus tells the crowd to beware of the scribes (vs 35-40)

Describe what the scribes loved.

And what does Jesus say some of their behavior is?

What will they receive because of this?

Think of this conversation with the scribe about the greatest commandments, noting how Jesus questions the scribes' teaching immediately afterward, warning people to beware of them.

From this passage, what can you observe about looking good on the outside, to people, instead of to God?

Jesus always starts with your heart.

When He works in your heart first, good character and behavior will develop after a time. You don't have to be perfect to follow Jesus.

Jesus turns His attention to the treasury. (Verse 41-42)

What did the rich put in?

But what does Jesus say about the widow?

Think about what Jesus was just talking about, how the greatest commandment is to love the Lord your God with all your heart.

But it all starts with inviting Him in to do a work in your heart.

Dear sister, it is not all about following the rules or pleasing people, but about having a true, authentic relationship with Jesus Christ.

Do you want more of that in your life? If you do, tell the Lord how you feel. Ask Him to make Himself real to you, and to help you have a true, authentic relationship with Him, one that starts with the heart.

What truth about Jesus stood out to you from this passage?

John 14:9 says when you've seen Jesus, you've seen the Father. What does this show you about your Heavenly Father?

What's going on in your heart as you realize this?

Write or say a prayer receiving this truth about your Heavenly Father and asking Him to heal the places you've been hurt by father figures in your life.

Day 26

Read Mark 13:1-23

What does Jesus say about the temple stones? (Verse 2)

Some of the disciples ask the Lord privately about the end times. Jesus describes several things in the next few paragraphs.

What are we to take heed of, and why? (Verse 5-6)

What are we to do when we hear of wars and rumors of wars? (Verse 7)

And why?

162 CAROLYN RICE

What does Jesus say will happen in verse 8?

And what are these are the beginning of? (Verse 8)

Describe what will happen to the Lord's followers in the end times? (Verse 9)

For what reason will the Lord's people be brought before rulers and kings? (Verse 9)

Where must the gospel be preached? (Verse 10)

What is Jesus' direction to those who are arrested? (Verse 11)

Describe what Jesus says will happen in families. (Verse 12)

What is the promise in verse 13?

What does verse 19 say about tribulation?

Why has God chosen to shorten the days of the tribulation? (Verse 20)

Why do you think Jesus told of all these things beforehand?

When you read about the tribulation, or the beginning of sorrows, it can be scary to think about. Yet throughout talking of this Jesus gives direction and promises. Often, I have found that when I am walking through any storm of life, I find comfort from God's promises, and His direction helps to guide me every step of the way. When I am following Jesus, I never walk alone.

Some of the directions and promises you'll find in this section are:

Do not be troubled. (Verse 7)

You will give testimony (Verse 9)

You will be given what to say, and the Holy Spirit will speak through you. (Verse 11)

He who endures to the end will be saved. (Verse 13)

Pray. (Verse 18)

What do these verses speak to you about things you can do when you go through tough times or suffering?

What truth about Jesus stood out to you from this passage?

John 14:9 says when you've seen Jesus, you've seen the Father. What does this show you about your Heavenly Father?

What's going on in your heart as you realize this?

Write or say a prayer receiving this truth about your Heavenly Father and asking Him to heal the places you've been hurt by father figures in your life.

Day 27

Read Mark 13: 24-37

What happens after the tribulation? (Verse 24-25)

Write verse 26 here.

What will Jesus do when He comes? (Verse 27)

If you have accepted Jesus as your Lord and Savior, you are part of the elect.

So, what does this scripture say Jesus will do for *you* when He comes?

How will we know that the end times are near? (Verse 29)

Write verse 31 here.

What will by no means pass away?

Who is the only One who knows the time and hour of these things happening? (Verse 32)

What is Jesus' direction to us regarding these times? (Verse 33)

What does Jesus say this is like? (Verse 34)

What does He say to do again in verse 35?

Write verse 37 here.

The New International Version uses the words, "Be on guard! Be alert!" while the New King James version and King James use the word, "Watch."

How many times does Jesus tell us to watch or be on guard? (Verse 33-37)

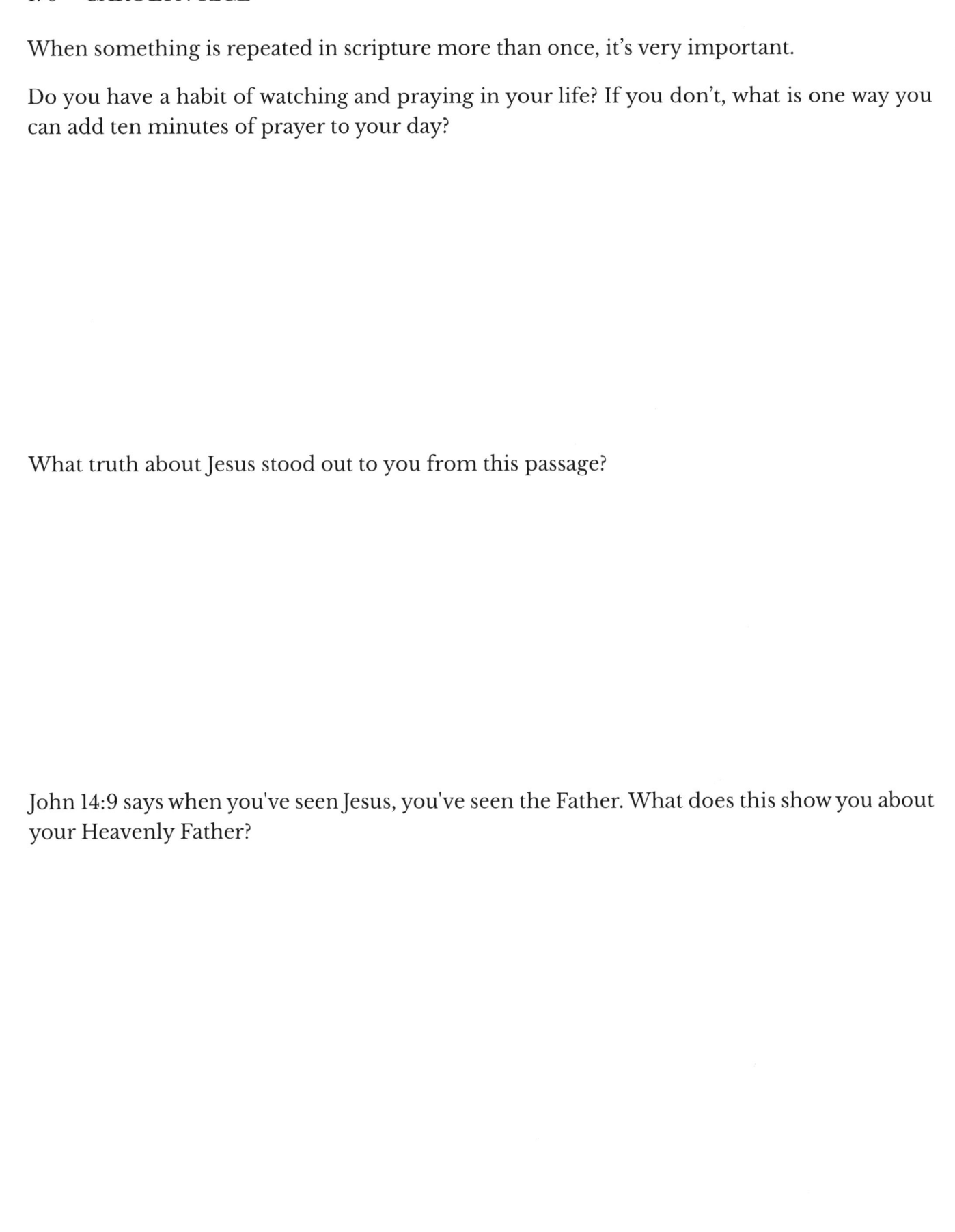

When something is repeated in scripture more than once, it's very important.

Do you have a habit of watching and praying in your life? If you don't, what is one way you can add ten minutes of prayer to your day?

What truth about Jesus stood out to you from this passage?

John 14:9 says when you've seen Jesus, you've seen the Father. What does this show you about your Heavenly Father?

What's going on in your heart as you realize this?

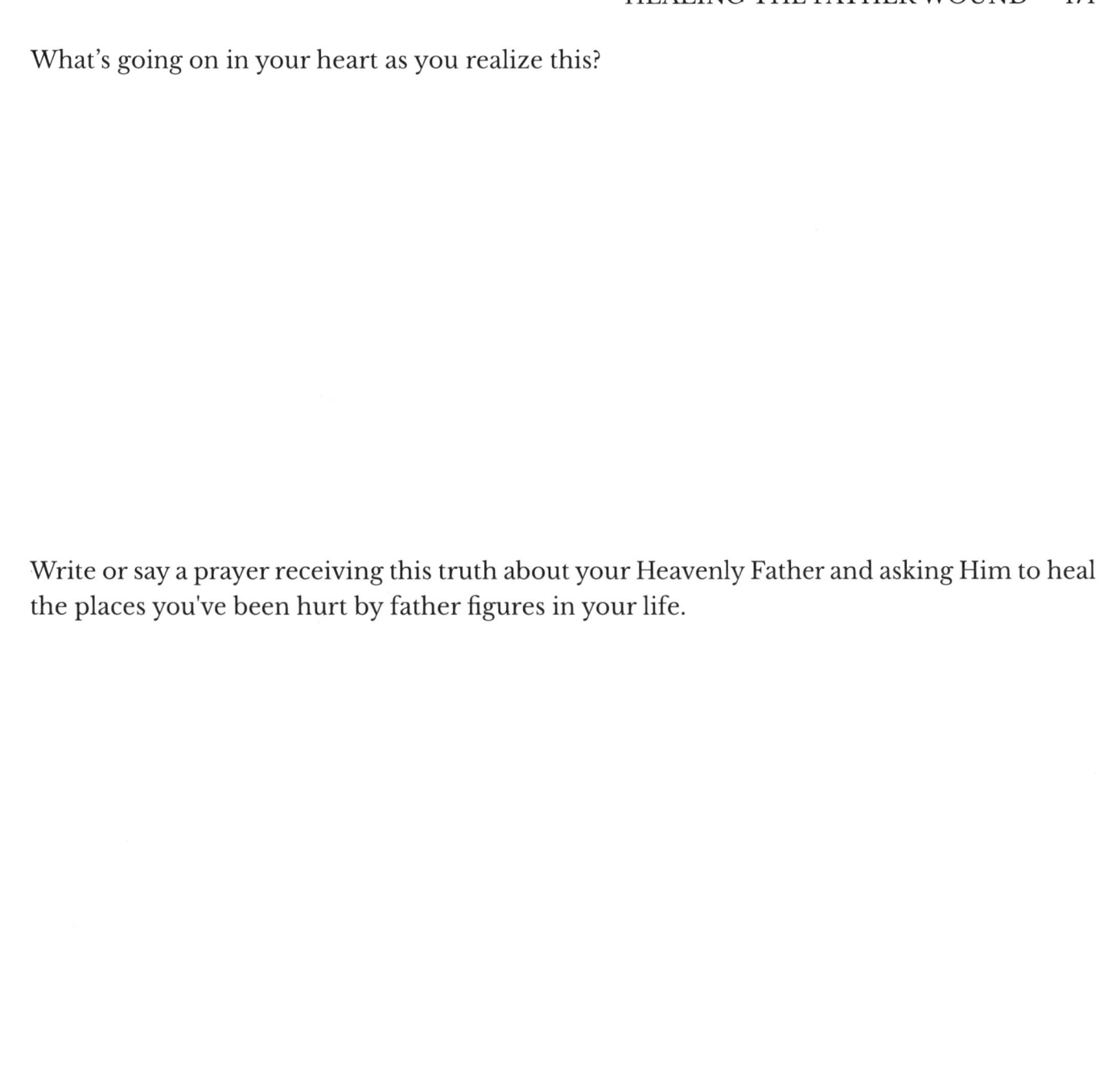

Write or say a prayer receiving this truth about your Heavenly Father and asking Him to heal the places you've been hurt by father figures in your life.

Day 28

Read Mark 14:1-31

Describe what the chief priests and scribes sought to do. (Verse 1)

Whose house was Jesus at in Bethany? (Verse 3)

Stop for a moment and think about that.

Who had invited Jesus to his house to spend time with Him?

And who wanted to stop Jesus' work altogether?

What do you think the difference between the two was?

Describe the woman and what she did in verse 3.

What was the response of some who saw this happen? (Verse 4-5)

And what was Jesus' response? (Verse 6-9)

Why did Judas go to the chief priests? (Verse 10)

What was he getting in return? (Verse 11)

What did the disciples ask Jesus? (Verse 12)

Describe who Jesus said to follow, and what they were to say to the owner of the house. (Verse 13-14)

When Jesus gave them the direction, what was the state of the room he said they would find? (Verse 15)

Has Jesus given you direction for your life? Explain.

Have you felt like you needed to fight the battles by yourself? Explain.

Describe again the state of the room He said they would find.

Write Jeremiah 29:11 here.

When the disciples found the room, what were they to do? (Verse 15)

When the disciples followed Jesus's direction, what did they find? (Verse 16)

When God gives you a promise, when He gives you a direction, do you think He will keep His word, or do you measure Him by your experiences with human beings?

Write Numbers 23:19 here.

As Jesus eats the last supper with His disciples, what does He say the bread is? (Verse 22)

And what does He say the cup is? (Verse 24)

What did they do before they left for the Mount of Olives? (Verse 26)

Before, we saw Jesus give the disciples direction on where to go and who to follow to find the upper room.

Now, He tells them they will all stumble that very night.

What does He say will happen after He has been raised? (Verse 27-28)

The disciples were about to walk into a very dark time, a time when it looked like all was lost.

Jesus was telling them they would stumble in their faith, but He would go before them.

Yet they didn't believe they could ever deny Him. What did they say to Him? (Verse 29-31)

Have you ever experienced a time where it looked like all was lost? Where it looked as if the enemy had won, and won big time? Explain.

Dear sister, what has Jesus spoken to your heart? What promise has He given you?

Keep walking.

keep going.

Do not quit.

For even if it looks dark for a time, Jesus is not done yet.

In the end, things will be just as He said.

In the end, you will walk into things fully prepared for you.

What truth about Jesus stood out to you from this passage?

John 14:9 says when you've seen Jesus, you've seen the Father. What does this show you about your Heavenly Father?

What's going on in your heart as you realize this?

Write or say a prayer receiving this truth about your Heavenly Father and asking Him to heal the places you've been hurt by father figures in your life.

Day 29

Read Mark 14:32-72

How is Jesus feeling in the garden of Gethsemane? (Verse 33-34)

What does He tell His disciples to do?

Describe what Jesus prayed. (Verse 35-36)

What did He find the disciples doing? (Verse 37)

Write verse 38 here.

What does Jesus pray again? (Verse 39)

And again, what does He find the disciples doing? (Verse 40)

HEALING THE FATHER WOUND 185

In your own words, summarize what Jesus says to His disciples. (Verse 41-42)

What was used as a signal by Jesus' betrayer? (Verse 44)

Write verse 50 here.

Have you ever felt betrayed by someone who was supposed to have your back? How did you feel?

Describe what Peter did. (Verse 54)

What happened when people tried to come against Jesus with false accusations? (Verse 55-61)

What accusation did they condemn Him for? (Verse 61-64)

Verse 65 describes the abuse heaped upon Jesus for who He was.

Name some things they did to Him.

Describe Peter's first denial. (Verse 66-68)

And his second denial. (Verse 69-70)

And the third. (Verse 71)

What happened when the rooster crowed the second time? (Verse 72)

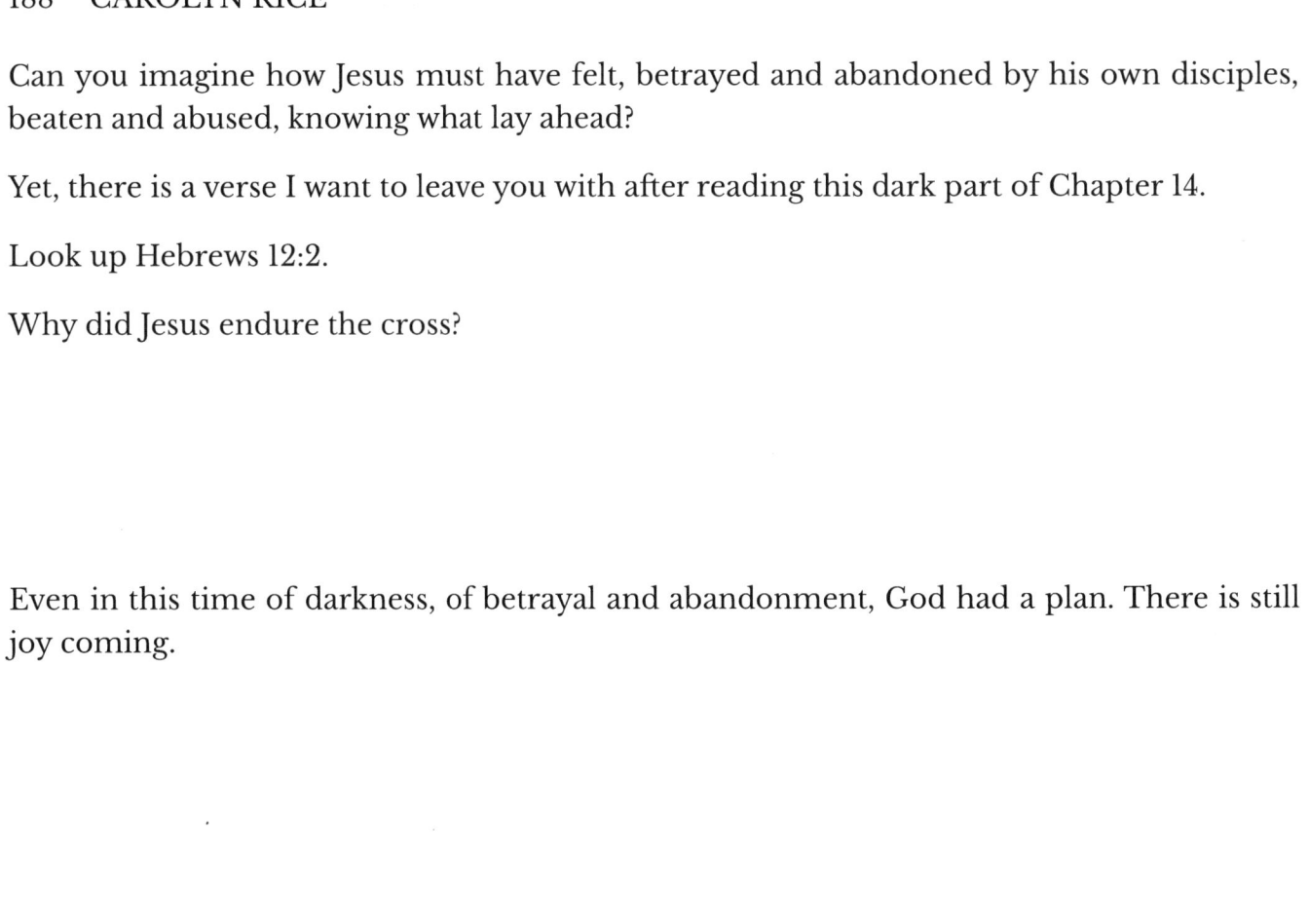

Can you imagine how Jesus must have felt, betrayed and abandoned by his own disciples, beaten and abused, knowing what lay ahead?

Yet, there is a verse I want to leave you with after reading this dark part of Chapter 14.

Look up Hebrews 12:2.

Why did Jesus endure the cross?

Even in this time of darkness, of betrayal and abandonment, God had a plan. There is still joy coming.

What truth about Jesus stood out to you from this passage?

John 14:9 says when you've seen Jesus, you've seen the Father. What does this show you about your Heavenly Father?

What's going on in your heart as you realize this?

Write or say a prayer receiving this truth about your Heavenly Father and asking Him to heal the places you've been hurt by father figures in your life.

Day 30

Read Mark 15:1-32

Why do you think Jesus wouldn't answer Pilate? (Verse 3-5)

Describe what usually happened at the feast? (Verse 6)

What was Barabbas's crime? (Verse 7)

Pilate knew why the chief priests handed Jesus over, what was the reason? (Verse 10)

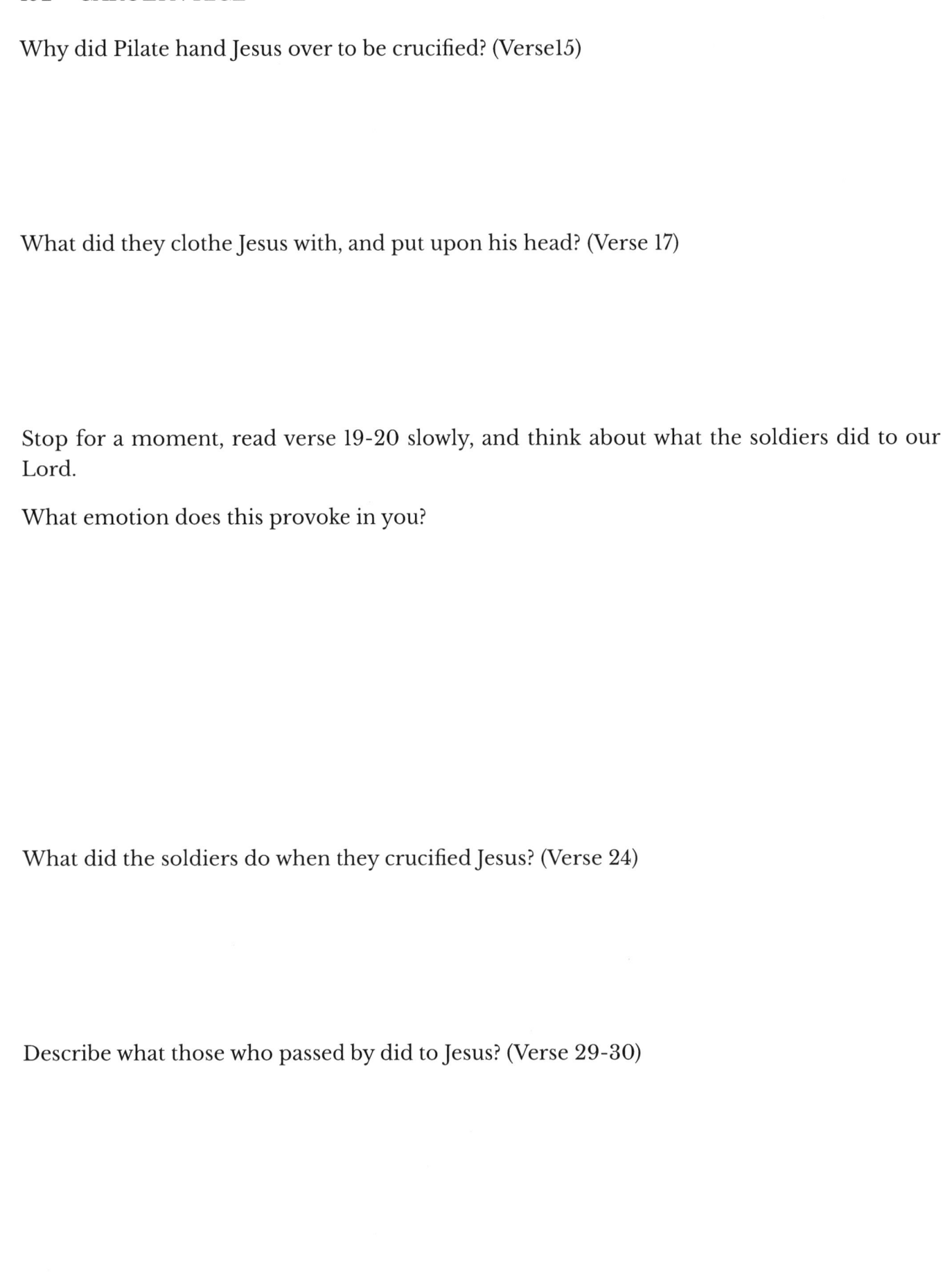

Why did Pilate hand Jesus over to be crucified? (Verse 15)

What did they clothe Jesus with, and put upon his head? (Verse 17)

Stop for a moment, read verse 19-20 slowly, and think about what the soldiers did to our Lord.

What emotion does this provoke in you?

What did the soldiers do when they crucified Jesus? (Verse 24)

Describe what those who passed by did to Jesus? (Verse 29-30)

HEALING THE FATHER WOUND 193

The chief priests wanted Him to come off the cross. Why? (Verse 32)

Yet God had another plan.

Dear sister, when things look the darkest, when you're going through terrible heartache and pain, when you just don't understand, remember, it is in that time, God still has a plan.

He has not abandoned you.

He has not forgotten you.

You are not alone.

What truth about Jesus stood out to you from this passage?

John 14:9 says when you've seen Jesus, you've seen the Father. What does this show you about your Heavenly Father?

What's going on in your heart as you realize this?

Write or say a prayer receiving this truth about your Heavenly Father and asking Him to heal the places you've been hurt by father figures in your life.

Day 31

Read Mark 15: 33-47

Describe what Jesus cried out on the cross. (Verse 34)

What happened after Jesus breathed His last? (Verse 37)

What did the centurion say?

Who came to ask for the body of Jesus? (43)

When he was granted Jesus' body, what did he do? (Verse 46)

Who was watching all of this happen? (Verse 47)

Dear sister, if you stop reading here, it looks as if evil has won.

Can you imagine how the disciples must have felt?

Betrayal, murder, hope destroyed.

Jesus had told them about this, but even when you know something is going to happen, are you ever really ready for it?

If you never turned the page, or never went on to the next chapter, you wouldn't know the victory God has planned. You wouldn't know the end of the story.

Can't we sometimes do that in our own lives?

We see that darkness has had its victory, and there we lay in the dust and ashes; Hopes dashed, trust destroyed, hearts broken.

You can choose to stay in those ashes, in that place of grief and mourning, or you can ask Jesus to help you rise from the ashes and turn the page.

Because, sister, God is not done with your story yet.

If you've been in those ashes, I invite you to you pray with me, asking Jesus to help you turn the page, then write the rest of your prayer below.

Father God, where darkness has reigned, where it seems like all is lost and hope has been destroyed, I cry out to you. I want to come out of these ashes, Lord.

I want to see your restoration in my life. I want to experience your victory, and I want hope to rise within me once again.

Lord, help me turn the page and watch the darkness and ashes be blown away by Your very breath.

Write the rest of your prayer here:

In Jesus' name, amen.

What truth about Jesus stood out to you from this passage?

John 14:9 says when you've seen Jesus, you've seen the Father. What does this show you about your Heavenly Father?

What's going on in your heart as you realize this?

Write or say a prayer receiving this truth about your Heavenly Father and asking Him to heal the places you've been hurt by father figures in your life.

Day 32

Read Mark 16:1-11

In chapter 15, we watched as Jesus was laid in the tomb.

An entire day passes.

The sabbath.

Can you imagine what the disciples and women who followed Jesus must have felt that sabbath? The heartache. Their beloved Jesus has been murdered.

All hope is lost.

Now we arrive in chapter 16.

What do Mary Magdalene and Mary the mother of James do in verse 1?

What did they say among themselves? (Verse 3)

And what did they find? (Verse 4)

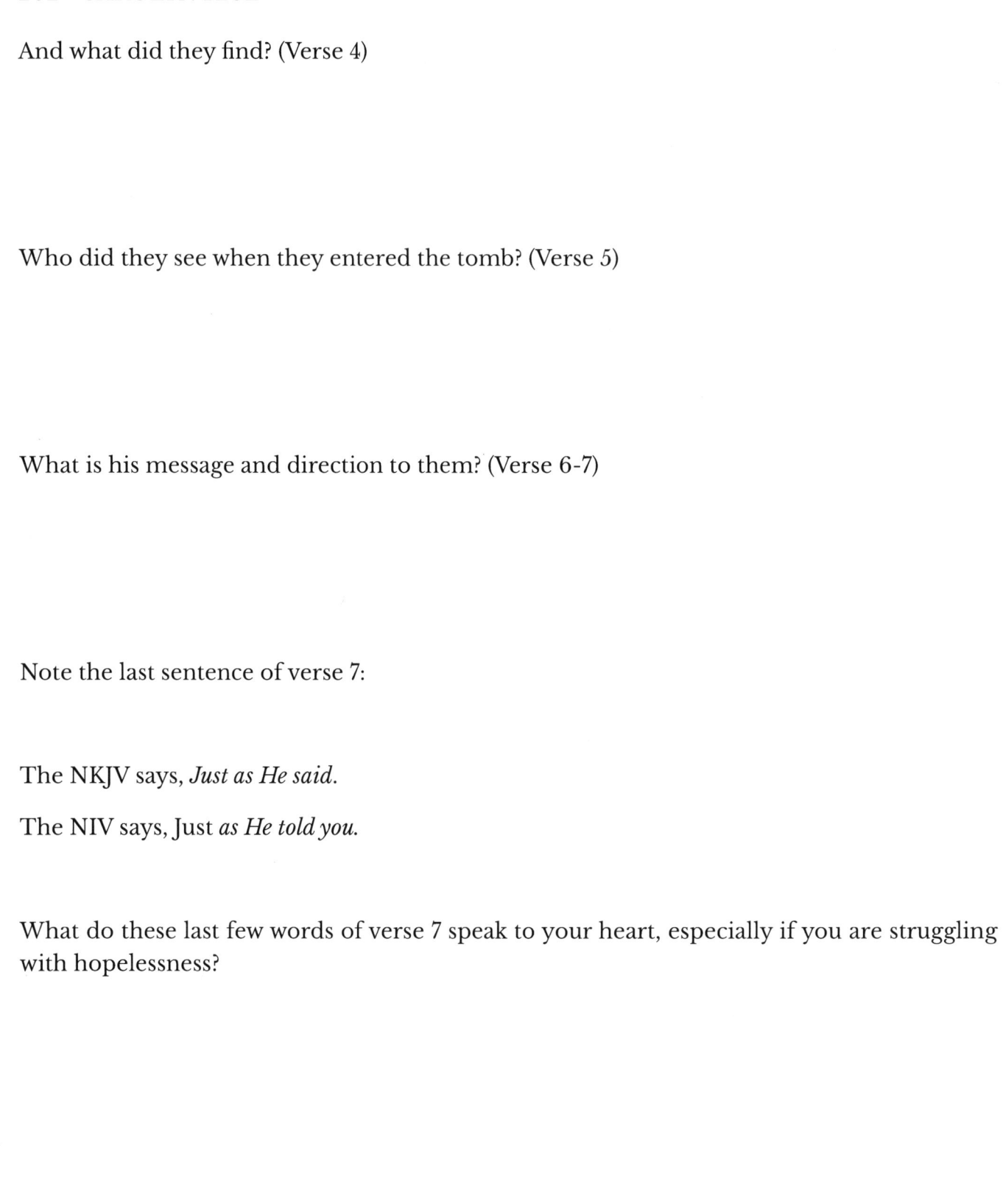

Who did they see when they entered the tomb? (Verse 5)

What is his message and direction to them? (Verse 6-7)

Note the last sentence of verse 7:

The NKJV says, *Just as He said*.

The NIV says, *Just as He told you*.

What do these last few words of verse 7 speak to your heart, especially if you are struggling with hopelessness?

What was the reaction of the two women? (Verse 8)

Who did Jesus appear to first? (Verse 9)

Describe what He had done for her.

What happened when she told the others she'd seen the risen Lord? (10-11)

The disciples were wracked with grief and hurting so badly. They knew their beloved Jesus was dead.

So, when someone came with great news, they couldn't bring themselves to believe.

Have you ever been in this place? Explain.

You have seen the enemy's work with your own eyes. It seems your whole world has fallen apart, and you're afraid to even hope again.

Dear daughter of the King, God still has a plan.

Do not give up hope when it seems all is lost.

Do not give up on God.

For even when you can't see it, His plan is still in motion.

What truth about Jesus stood out to you from this passage?

John 14:9 says when you've seen Jesus, you've seen the Father. What does this show you about your Heavenly Father?

What's going on in your heart as you realize this?

Write or say a prayer receiving this truth about your Heavenly Father and asking Him to heal the places you've been hurt by father figures in your life.

Day 33

Read Mark 16:12-20

Jesus appeared again to two disciples. What happened when they told the rest? (Verse 12-13)

Later, He appeared to the eleven. What did Jesus rebuke? (verse14)

What did Jesus say to do in verse 15?

What signs will follow those who believe? (Verse 17-18)

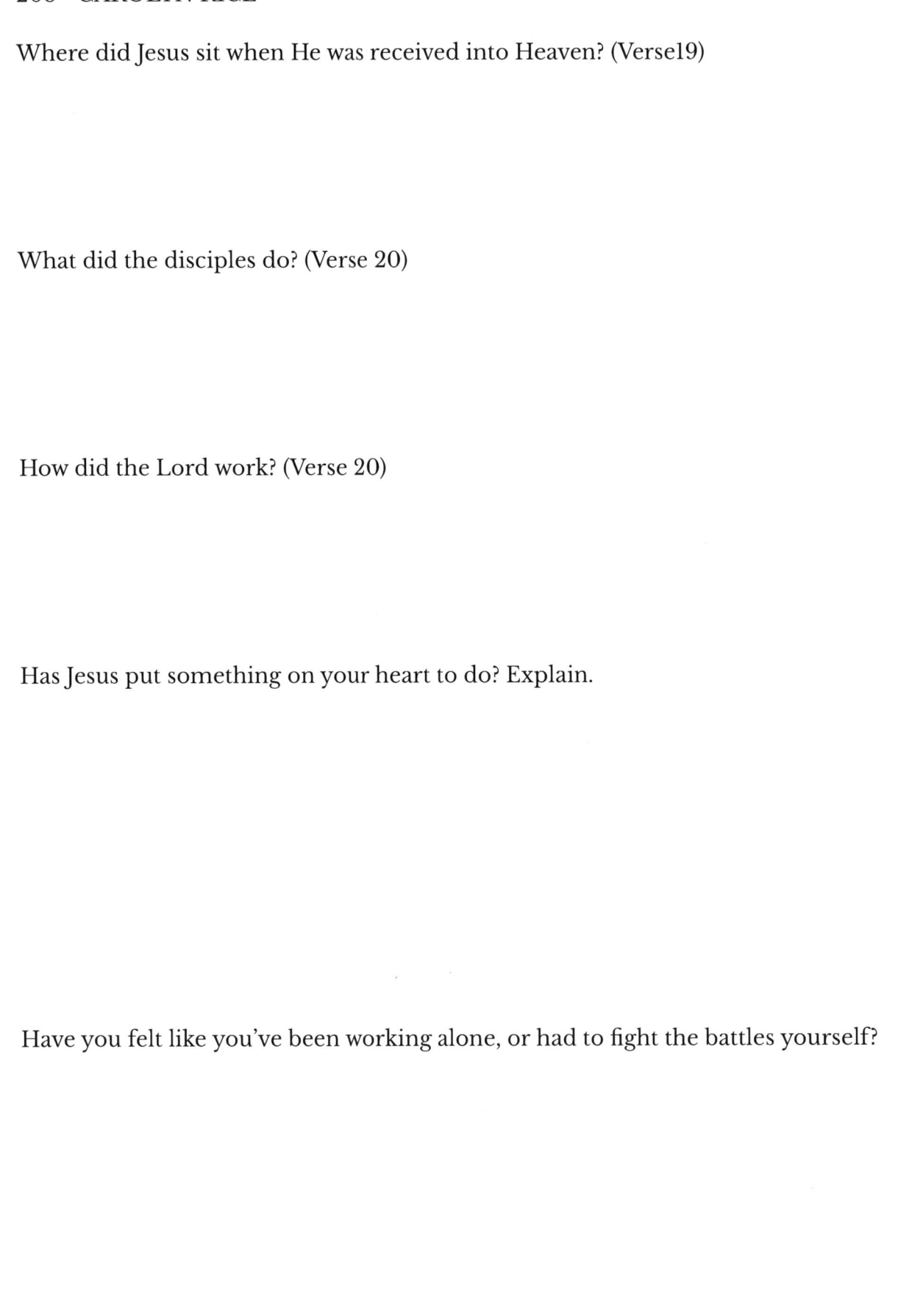

Where did Jesus sit when He was received into Heaven? (Verse 19)

What did the disciples do? (Verse 20)

How did the Lord work? (Verse 20)

Has Jesus put something on your heart to do? Explain.

Have you felt like you've been working alone, or had to fight the battles yourself?

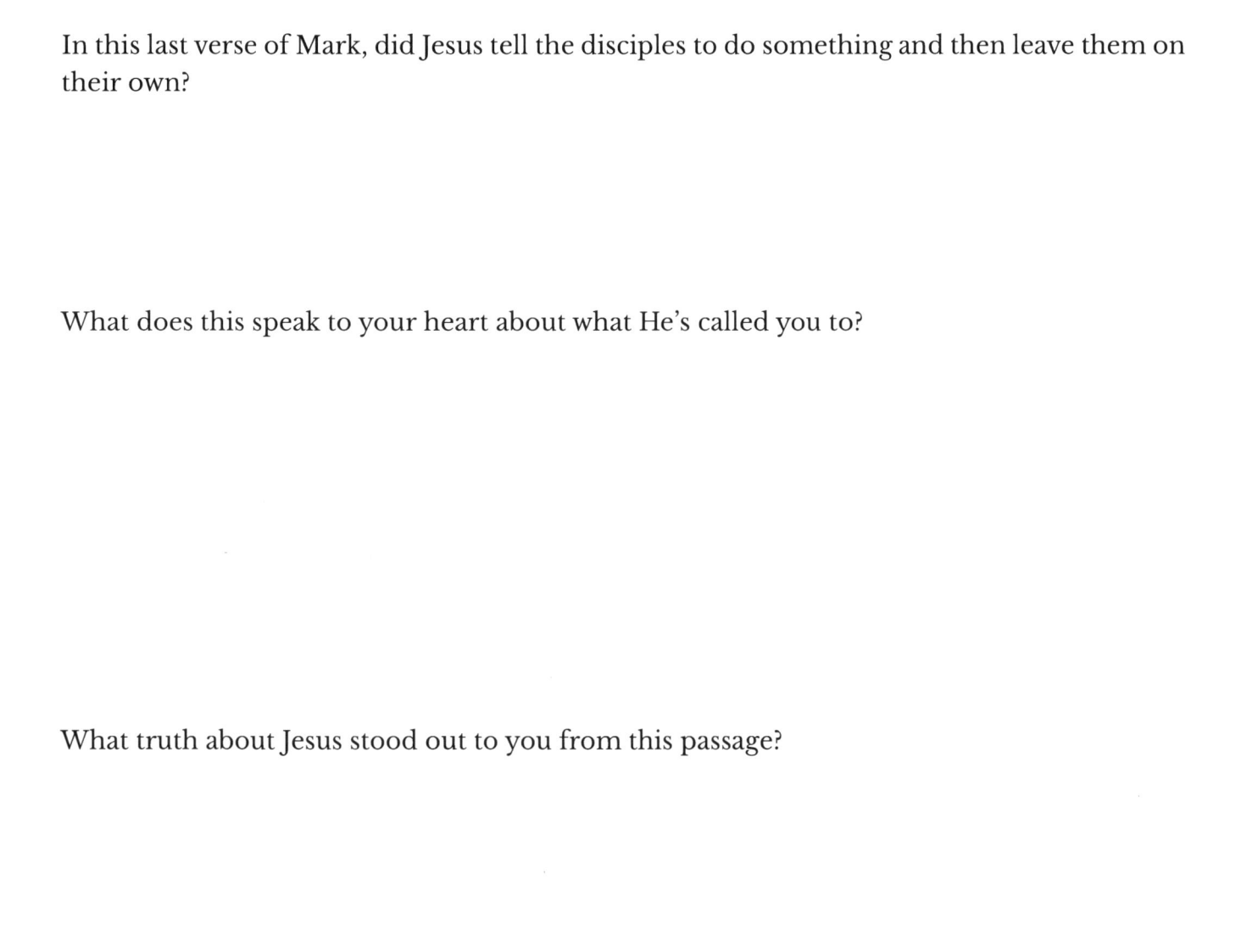

In this last verse of Mark, did Jesus tell the disciples to do something and then leave them on their own?

What does this speak to your heart about what He's called you to?

What truth about Jesus stood out to you from this passage?

John 14:9 says when you've seen Jesus, you've seen the Father. What does this show you about your Heavenly Father?

What's going on in your heart as you realize this?

Write or say a prayer receiving this truth about your Heavenly Father and asking Him to heal the places you've been hurt by father figures in your life.

Have you struggled with rejection, fear, or a broken heart?

Author Carolyn Rice, a survivor of abuse, struggled with all of these and more. There were times she felt alone and isolated, like the only one who understood at all was God.

God Sees Your Tears is a collection of prayers calling out to God for help with discouragement, anger, shame, bad memories and more. Each prayer comes with a scripture to find comfort from God's Word.

You don't have to feel alone anymore.

Subscribe to Carolyn's Newsletter and download your free gift at CarolynsBooks.com today.

Also By Carolyn Rice

Lord, Heal My Heart: A Devotional

Lord, Help Me Forgive: An 8-Week Journey through Forgiveness

Loved by the Father: A Women's Bible Study through John and First John

Did You Love This Bible Study?

Please leave a review where you purchased it.

About the Author

Carolyn Rice holds an Associate Degree in Biblical studies and has worked in several aspects of ministry, including teaching Cleansing Stream Seminars, and serving as the Alumni Director for Seattle Bible College. Carolyn hosts the Abide in Jesus podcast and has written several books on finding healing in Christ. She is a survivor of abuse and wants to share the healing she found in Jesus with others.

She has two grown children, one granddaughter, and lives with her husband and two dogs in Granite Falls, Washington.

Find out more about Carolyn and her books at CarolynsBooks.com

Prayer for Salvation

Jesus, I accept you as my Savior. I believe You died on the cross and rose again to free me from my sins. I accept Your free gift of forgiveness now. I invite You into my heart and my life, and I choose to follow You, living my life for You from this day forward.

Help me to grow and mature in You.

In Your name I pray, amen.

Resources

*"G3850 - parabolē - Strong's Greek Lexicon (kjv)." Blue Letter Bible. Web. 1 Sep, 2022. <https://www.blueletterbible.org/lexicon/g3850/kjv/tr/0-1/>.

Made in United States
Troutdale, OR
03/01/2025